Seasons of the
Feminine Divine

CYCLE C

Seasons of the Feminine Divine

Christian Feminist Prayers for the Liturgical Cycle

CYCLE C

— ❧ —

MARY KATHLEEN SPEEGLE SCHMITT

CROSSROAD • NEW YORK

1994

The Crossroad Publishing Company
370 Lexington Avenue, New York, NY 10017

Printed in the United States of America

Library of Congress Cataloging-in-Publication Data
(Revised for vol. 2)
Schmitt, Mary Kathleen Speegle.
    Seasons of the feminine divine.

    Vol. [1] based on Cycle B of the Common
lectionary.
    Includes bibliographical references and
index.
    Contents: [1. Without special title] —
[2] Cycle C.
    1. Church year—Prayer-books and devotions
—English. 2. Women—Religious life.
I. Title.
BV30.S323   1993   264'.12'082   93-588
    ISBN 0-8245-1443-2 (v. 2)

In memory of my great-aunts:

Nona, Treasure, Betty, Kate, Mary, and Lily,
with love and gratitude for their earthiness,
the strength of their woman-endurance, and their wisdom;

and dedicated to my aunts:

Eleanor, Juanita, Mary, Mae, and Alma,
who revealed to me much of women's experience in life,
opening my eyes both to our woundedness
and our capacity for goodness and beauty.

Contents

*Prayers for Pentecost and the Sundays in Ordinary Time
from May 8 to July 2*

Introduction

—— ❦ ——

M ANY TIMES prayers say what we ought to believe. Rather than enabling us to open to the mystery of the Divine, they close down our imaginations with doctrinal statements or moral admonitions. The prayers in the series seek to be evocative, touching our hearts and minds with new perceptions of the Divine, who is far beyond human comprehension. In this second volume of *Seasons of the Feminine Divine,* I continue the exploration of Who the Holy One is, particularly in Her feminine aspect, and who it is She calls us to become, in Her image.

This volume of prayers is the second in a three-year cycle. The first volume was based on Cycle B of the Ecumenical Lectionary (Revised, Episcopal, Lutheran, Roman Catholic, and Anglican Church of Canada); the prayers in this book relate to Cycle C. In the introduction to the first volume I examined the reasons for seeking out the feminine Divine, the ways She has been present throughout Judeo-Christian tradition, the relationship of ancient Goddess religion to Judeo-Christian tradition, how the maleness of Jesus poses a problem for women of faith, and the narrative and poetic nature of the prayers in these cycles. In this volume I examine issues around the association of gender with our understanding of the Divine, the use of repetition in prayer images, the problem of stereotyping, and the importance of cyclical worship in spiritual formation.

Sources and Impact
of Male and Female Imagery

How did we develop gender connotations for the Divine in the first place? Many of us would be quick to say that the godhead is neither female nor male, and that the Holy One is infinitely beyond the limitations of human attributes with which we attempt to understand the Divine. It is important to consider what gender reference to the Divine is about. Where did it come from? Would it not be best to eliminate gender reference altogether? Why is it necessary to return to female names and images for the Divine?

The way images become part of our understanding of the Divine. In earliest time the Divine was seen as the Grandmother, the memory of a venerated elder-woman from the past activated as the people's belief that She was present in the contemporary moment. The female was seen as connected to the Divine because of her birth-giving powers, her seemingly miraculous connection to the Goddess of creation. It was only later that the connection between the male and procreation was recognized.[1] From that time there was a movement to view the female's inability to create children without a male as a weakness or a lack. The understanding developed that women were vessels only and had no active role in the producing of children.

When society was matriarchal, there was no confusion about whose child the heir was — she had clearly been born from a particular woman. In patriarchal society the identification was not so clear. Out of the male need to claim connection to the Divine through the producing of heirs, a system was devised to assure that the child was actually his.

The new system was not quickly embraced. Only through a long and often violent process of subduing women's prerogatives concerning children and their own sexual behavior were men able to gain ascendancy in the social structure. Now that men could have heirs, as women once had had, they saw their continuity with the future through their descendants as a "right" and "responsibility," deemed very important in many societies even today. Thus, the sexual ethic, which particularly affects women, developed from what was once understood as an exclusive women's right but became an exclusive men's right. The purpose of this ethic was to control access to the heirs. Its consequence was to rigidly control the lives of women and to restrict their freedom in a multitude of ways.

A central part of the move from matriarchal to patriarchal perceptions was that the Divine, understood as Creator, became seen as male rather than female, and the whole history of Hebrew religion advocated against "fertility cults" or the female way of seeing procreation and connection to the Divine. The result was the elimination of the female from the godhead, so that everything that had signified woman's connection with the Divine, such as menstruation and birthgiving powers, became seen as unclean and connected with evil. The Goddess myths of the ancient Middle East were adapted to give the Divine a male identity — as in the Judeo-Christian story where Adam gives birth to Eve from his rib, or the Greek myth in which Zeus gives birth from the side of his head in order to claim the divine procreative power.

In the new mythology the goddess symbol, the serpent, became identified as evil itself, Satan, so that one of the most important pictures of the Virgin Mary as redeemed woman shows her crushing the head of a snake, which in Goddess religion had represented the regenerative power of life. Thus the basic image in Christian religion for women is that of the woman subduing the Goddess within and of women, therefore, giving up their essential WomanWisdom[2] in order to serve the male need to identify his heirs and wield power through his right to have heirs. All of the legends in Christian tradition of slaying dragons or snakes or driving dragons out (as St. Patrick is said to have done in Ireland) have to do with eliminating female power and the essential feminine. In this way, women became estranged from themselves in the image of the Divine, estranged from the true nature of their own souls, and divided against each other in order to survive in dependence upon men. Estranged from one another, they became limited in their ability to support one another. "Femininity" became identified with images of weakness and docility and other characteristics of stress common in people forced into submission.[3] It is only fairly recently, after science revealed that women are more than "vessels" — that indeed through ovarian activity they play a dynamic part in the creation of children — that attitudes have, very slowly, been modified to recognize both parents as equal in the creative process.

The move to a balance of male and female images. As we reflect on the historical process, we can have a certain sympathy for men, who were excluded from divine symbolism in ancient times because they were seen as inferior, and we can understand their rage; at the same time, it is very difficult to accept the centuries of violent oppression of women by which men gained ascendancy in the theological and political realms. The task that is before us is the recognition of our equality before God/dess. Although both women and men play vital roles in producing offspring, we no longer tie our understanding of the Divine in a literal fashion to biological function. Women initiate great intellectual ideas and movements, new methods for seeking justice, and great works of art. Men give birth to acts of love and tenderness, as in child rearing or nursing or counselling, which support and nurture people and attempt to enhance life. Both women and men participate in the great mystery and creativity of life that encompasses all things.

One might suggest, then, that it is better to eliminate sexual reference to the Divine altogether. However, until the feminine is revalued and women are seen as valuable in the image of the Divine, we are left with an imbalance of understanding of the godhead, and justice for women is still lacking. Neutral names or images for the Divine would be heard as masculine, and women would still be viewed in the image of the Divine in some secondary kind of way.

The Use of Repetition in Establishing Male Imagery for the Divine

How is it that the image of "Father" has become so strong in the symbolic system of Christendom — to the extent that thealogian Sallie McFague suggests that this image has become idolatrous in our time?[4] First of all, the metaphor was biblical — starting in the Hebrew scriptures[5] and developed by Jesus to express the intimate connection between the Divine and humankind in contrast with titles such as "Lord" and "Almighty." The Abba-Father image is poignant with tenderness and understanding and love. In this context the image of "Father" is deeply moving and transforming for the persons praying. This biblical image used and taught by Jesus himself continues to make a deep impression on people of the Christian faith.

Another way, however, that the image of "Father" has become dominant has been through societal influence. Although ancient religion in the Middle East was matriarchal and full of female images, particularly images suggesting women's connection to the Divine through their birth-giving powers, by the time Hebrew scripture opened, there had been a rapid and violent move to patriarchal society and religious symbol in which fathers became the absolute authority in a family social organization. Roman civilization, as well, had become patriarchal. The role of the father in society became part of people's perception of the role of the Divine, so that the image retained the earlier connotation of a Deity who

exerts power over others rather than the picture of an intimate and sustaining Father as portrayed in the teachings of
Jesus.

Jesus' view of the image of Father posed a radical challenge to Judaism and later to Christianity. It is important
to understand that the father in the parable of the Prodigal Son is a fool. No self-respecting father in that society
would have taken his son back after that son had wasted
his inheritance recklessly. The real prodigal in the story is
the father, the one who did not count the material cost and
gave love as though the supply were inexhaustible. This is
not the authoritative, almighty father of patriarchy; this is
a father who is wholly parabolic, or surprising in a turn-
the-world-upside-down sense — the father who unexpectedly
understands, cares, loves, and sustains despite the wayward-
ness of the child. While this aspect of the Father metaphor is
one way we understand the Divine today, the cultural idea
of the patriarch with divine right and sole authority still
controls the perception of this image in the minds of many
believers.

Because of the importance of the father in patriarchal society and the desire of the male hierarchy to maintain control
in the social and political arena, this metaphor became more
and more used. The more the name was used, the deeper
it moved into the consciousness of the believers. As society
influenced the Christian Church, the Church reinforced the
patriarchal structure of society and the roles of dominance
and submission of men and women in that structure.

The Importance of Repetition of Female Images

Think, for instance, what might have happened in society
if the metaphor "Mother Jesus" had been reinforced in-
stead of "Father." "Mother Jesus" is an image that stems
from the earliest time in the Church and was particularly

strong among the mystics in the Middle Ages. It was an androgynous image of nurturing and tenderness whereas in the mainstream of church life, the view of Jesus was moving to that of absolute monarch, the ascended Prince seated at the right hand of God the (Almighty) Father, an image that fed the monarchies of Europe in their quest for power and continued to restrict the role and self-image of women.

The feminine became more and more invested in that which is not divine — in earth, in fallible Church (as contrasted with infallible God), in the Virgin Mary (human rather than divine), and particularly in a very repressed understanding of the Virgin seen as a woman who submitted to impregnation by the Father out of a deep reverence and obedience, produced a male heir, and stayed in the background. Women, of course, were instructed to model their lives after this repressed, obedient picture of womanhood. At the same time there was a popular refusal to repress Mary in this way; increasingly the people venerated her as higher than human. This veneration of Mary caused some concern in the Church because Mary, not seen as divine in church doctrine, was perceived as divine in the minds of the people. The leaders of the Reformation, therefore, removed mariology from centrality in the devotion of people altogether. As a result this image of womanhood was less connected with divinity than it had been before in the popular mind, and "Father" became more emphasized than ever until, in the time of the Enlightenment, "Father" became almost *the* name for the Divine.

Had "Mother Jesus" remained a major symbol of the Church's understanding of the Divine, might not civilization have developed differently? It is only recently that human fathers have been able to regain their prodigal natures, showing their love in almost "wasteful" ways, so that their love again is seen as tender and gentle, whereas for a long time

love was seen as requiring duty, and mercy was a kind of
royal dispensation carefully meted out to those who were
deserving.

The images that are repeated the most are the ones that
have been strong in the culture that surrounds a religion. The
images that get lost are the underside or shadow side of the
divine personality. These lost or less emphasized images tell
us about the Divine as much as the dominant images do,
but they are not part of our deep consciousness because we
do not hear them repeated over and over in the prayer and
teaching of the Church.

The prayers in *Seasons of the Feminine Divine*, therefore,
repeat certain female images, although often with variations
in presentation, in order to move us from intellectual play toward a deep consciousness of Womangod. The images used
in the first volume of *Seasons* that parabolically connect traditional female roles with the Divine — linking femaleness
with nature, giving birth, serving as a midwife, mothering,
cooking, housekeeping, sewing, weaving, etc. — reappear, although in different trappings, in this second volume: Mother
of Creation, Tree, Star, Turtledove, Water, Divine Midwife,
Weaver, Divine (female) Potter, Provider of Bread, Quilter,
etc. The image of a Mother mourning the loss of her children
is also carried from the first to this second volume in Christa
Most Sorrowful, Grief-stricken Mother, Weeping Woman,
and Mother of the Oppressed. In this way the themes from
the first volume are carried on in the present, sometimes using the same title and more often changing the words slightly.
If we do not worship the Divine through constant repetition
of these images, our understanding of the Divine as Womangod will not deepen, and the transformation we seek in using
these prayers will have minimal value in our spiritual formation. It is important to move from an elementary exploration
of a variety of images to the kind of deep consciousness we
have had for more traditional images such as "Father" and

"Lord," recognizing that at the same time, variety in images enhances our sense and understanding of the Divine.

Revaluing the Feminine: The Problem of Stereotyping

In this series I have used two approaches in order to facilitate the opening up of our imaginations to the feminine Divine: (1) I have written prayers that value the feminine as we know it in the symbolic system of Western civilization, and (2) I have created images of the feminine that are assertive and challenge the old view of what "femininity" is. The sources of the images are from within scripture, although often they are derived intuitively from what is said or perhaps not said. This approach has the difficulty of creating a tension between the female experience in past centuries and what we consider today to be stereotypical. For instance, on All Saints' Day in the first volume of *Seasons* I based the prayer on my memory of my Great-aunt Nona when I was a small child. In this prayer I am remembering Aunt Nona in the big garden out behind the farmhouse where she lived in rural Texas. As far as I know, she tended this garden by herself; Uncle Davis took care of the livestock and also worked off the farm. To me this garden was a magical place where we followed Aunt Nona through towering corn and asparagus, helping her harvest green beans or peas that she would prepare for dinner. I remember her, for the most part, wearing an apron made of flour sacking, which had to be starched and ironed. She would wear an apron in the garden as well as in the kitchen, where she canned much of the food she grew and where she made good things for us to eat. The image is based on a real person in a historical moment; yet in a feminist prayer a portrayal of this type can be perceived as stereotypical. My intention in using such an image is to re-value the work that Aunt Nona and other women did, and to honor them. If these volumes were to include masculine images of the Divine, then perhaps I could balance images that seem stereotypical by adding pictures of men in the kitchen wearing aprons. However, since I have limited the prayers to female images, I cannot create this kind of balance, which may leave some readers dissatisfied with time-bound images of women that today are perceived as stereotypical. The way I hope to offset the stereotypical has been through the development of images that in the past were considered masculine but in the prayer image are fleshed out with female experience, such as the images of Inventor and Architect in this volume, and images in which women are strong and wise. In addition, I have added a number of laments to the opening prayers, which allow for more expression of human suffering and the experience of the oppression of women and other groups of people.

The Seasons: Continuing the Spiral Dance

Cyclical and linear worship and spiritual formation. A major difference between ancient Goddess religion and Judeo-Christian religion has been the shift from worship based on the cycle of nature, with which women had affinity through their own bodily rhythm, to a linear, historical understanding of reality. While the story of Judeo-Christian tradition has great value for us in our worship and understanding of the faith, emphasis on history and a linear movement toward the End Time are inadequate by themselves to help us in our faith formation. We need a renewal of the cyclical aspect of our faith reality. In some branches of the Christian church seasons are observed and celebrated. Through focusing on selected biblical and doctrinal emphases as we learn and pray, we deepen in the faith. As we move through the cycles year after year, our knowledge of the Divine and of the community of Christ deepens. Each time we circle, hopefully we grow, while at the same time, much of what is there is missed. So we circle again, pick up more on each round, and continue. Feminist Christians claim the Goddess image of spiral motion to describe faith formation that is both linear and cyclical. The spiral motion connects our participation in the faith story more intimately with personal growth in the experience of Love and our own capacity to love others.

The culmination of the cycle happens at Easter, the ritual of death and rebirth that restores in a much deeper way the feminine cyclical nature of our religious experience. Through the Christ event the Judeo-Christian tradition recovered more deeply the depth and intensity of the female religious cycle, while not limiting the onward movement of the ongoing Story.

A Female Version of Life as Movement through Death and Resurrection. In the first volume of *Seasons* I emphasized the stages of women's experience from the time in the womb to the time of death. In this volume I am connecting the seasons to the rhythm of the liturgical cycle with its experiential movement through birth, life, death, and resurrection. This emphasis on the feminine dimension of death and birth was not new with Christianity. There are many stories of death and resurrection in Goddess religion as well as in other religions and cultures. Judaism had its own cyclical rituals, such as the Feast of the Tabernacles. These myths can give us insight into the particular feminine dimension the Christ event brings to the Judeo-Christian tradition and how Jesus' death and resurrection herald the return of this female dimension into our consciousness.

For me, the discovery of Sylvia Brinton Perera's *Descent to the Goddess: A Way of Initiation for Women* opened my imagination about the Christ event in a way I had not expected. Perera writes that there are many myths of the goddess descending and of going down to the goddess: the Japanese Izanami, the Greek Kore-Persephone, Roman Psy-

che, and the fairy-tale heroines who go to Mother Hulda or
Baba Yaha or the gingerbread house witch. In *Descent to the
Goddess* she is writing about the most ancient of these myths
available to us. This myth is about Inanna, the Sumerian
"queen of heaven and earth."[6] In this poem Inanna, a sky
goddess, sets out to go to the underworld, requesting Ninshubur, "her trusted female executive," to obtain help from
the father gods if she does not return in three days.[7]

In order to reach the underworld she must go through
seven gates. Told of Inanna's coming, the queen of the underworld, Ereshkigal, is very angry and instructs the gatekeeper
to see that Inanna goes through the requirements of any-
one coming to the underworld: each must leave behind their
worldly possessions and enter naked and humble. As Inanna
goes through the seven gates, she is judged by seven judges
and in the end killed by Ereshkigal. Her body is then pegged
to the wall where it rots. When Inanna does not return in
three days, Ninshubur appeals to Enlil, the highest god of
sky and earth, and to Nanna, the moon god (Inanna's father),
both of whom refuse to help her. However, Enki, god of waters and wisdom, comes to Inanna's aid and sends the food
and water of life to her by means of two mourners who comfort Ereshkigal. In gratitude Ereshkigal gives them Inanna's
body. Inanna then returns through the seven gates, reclaiming
a piece of her clothing at each one. Required by Ereshkigal
to send a substitute or scapegoat for herself, she chooses Dumuzi, her main consort or lover, who has not mourned her
absence. Dumuzi flees with the aid of his sister, Geshtinanna,
and in the end Inanna requires that each of them spend a half
of each year in the underworld. She is able to achieve this
act with the power she has gained from Ereshkigal and her
experience of death.

Perera sees in this myth the ability of women who have become alienated from their inner female power to return to
their own deep femininity. In order to do this, we need to

strip ourselves of the thought patterns of patriarchal thinking through which we have become separated from ourselves as connected with the Feminine Divine and in which we must inevitably hate ourselves, although this hatred is at such a deep level that we are most often unaware of it. Rather than being our Self, we are "good, nurturant mothers and wives; sweet, docile agreeable daughters; gently supportive or bright achieving partners."[8] We are estranged from the deep feminine power of our foremothers in ancient times — and with good cause, as many foremothers from Hebrew times to the present have been either executed as witches or humiliated and exiled when they have dared to reclaim and exert their female power. In order to avoid the dangers of this innate power, "we mutilate, depotentiate, silence, and enrage ourselves trying to compress our souls into [the patriarchal collective model]."[9] Inanna is the repressed feminine, the female entity who is disconnected from her true Self and, as queen of heaven and earth, is, before her descent to the goddess Ereshkigal, remarkably similar to the Virgin Mary, another representation of the repressed feminine (although Mary holds potential for some recovery of female wholeness if seen in a different way). These female images that have not met and connected with their "dark" or "deep" side, with their inner power that comes of being in their bodies and whole, lead us away from ourselves rather than to our Self in Christ.

In *Seasons of the Feminine Divine* I have drawn on the meaning of the Inanna-Ereshkigal myth by looking at the "dark" side of female experience, particularly in which women are abused and battered. With the perspective of this myth I see Christ crucified in each rape or battering, whether physical or psychological. While it is true that these violent forms of oppression are appalling and evil, it is also true that once we have been nailed, so to speak, on the wall of hell, the anger and hatred that we have heretofore focused on ourselves as inferior beings now unleashes in us as power that carries us to identify the evil we have experienced and empowers us to claim our own humanity and Womangod for ourselves. Moving toward wholeness within ourselves, we work for the wholeness of humankind and all creation. The coming of Christ in Jesus marks the return of our consciousness of the feminine Divine, but not only because of the story's similarity to the Sumerian myth. When the Divine enters creation in the human Jesus, we are once again given the image of God/dess operating from within our nature as well as transcending our nature. In Jesus' baptism, the primary symbol of the Goddess, the dove, returns to major significance in the human symbolic system. The pentecostal images of being born again reconnect us with the reality of the birth-giving Goddess and the reality that we are one with nature and that the Divine resides in and with us. The Christ event — the sequence of Jesus' death, descent into hell (the land of no return), and resurrection — restores us to the basic power of God/dess as connected with our bodies and our earthly nature. Jesus' statement that if we do not take up the cross we will not find life (Matthew 10:38) makes it clear that a return to the feminine Divine is a necessary part of the spiritual journey for both women and men.

The Relationship of the First and Second Volumes

In this volume of *Seasons*, I have expanded some of the concepts used in the first and have moved into images that go beyond the sense of those in the first volume. The chaotic side of the Divine (Womangod as Flood and Wilderness, Storm-Goddess, Liberator) is given a little more place in the second volume: Ecstatic Woman, Whirlwind Spirit, Fire of Justice, Tempestuous Goddess, and Thief Who Comes in the Night. The image of Womangod as Lover (Beloved One, Persistent Lover, Lover of Our Bodies and Souls, and Lover of Creation) is continued in the prayers "Friend of the Cosmos," "Infinite Love," and "Lover of All"; but in this second volume there is more emphasis on Divine Love as co-suffering (Shekinah as the One who accompanied the Israelites into exile, Christa Most Sorrowful, Woman Crucified, Battered Woman, Vulnerable One, Assaulted Goddess, and Sister of Color) — Christ seen in the suffering of women. Wisdom themes (Root of Wisdom, Mother Wisdom, Divine Healing Woman, and Wise Grandmother) are continued in Sophia, Mother Wisdom, Emergent Wisdom, Source of Wisdom, Womangod as Healer, and Elder-woman, but there is more emphasis on the wisdom of the Divine in images such as Seer of the End of Time, Grandmother, and Old Woman, images that allow us to accept ourselves as part of nature and yet carry us beyond simple physical reality to wholeness.

The first volume paid particular attention to portrayal of the Divine in images of womanhood in traditional roles (inversion of meaning from the mundane to the divine), biblical nature images, traditional biblical images such as Wisdom and images drawn from Sarah and Mary Magdalene and other women, and moved toward some themes of liberation. This second volume attempts to express roles that have normally been heard as masculine in feminine terms, such as Manager, Inventor, Priest(ess) of Earth and Sky, and Architect, that is, to give images we have seen as masculine their female dimension. I attempt also to portray Jesus in a role subservient to a woman, washing her feet, not biblical in a literal sense but derivative of the essence of the Maundy Thursday washing of feet. Images drawn from ancient Goddess religion but put into a Christian context are more present in this second volume, for instance, in the dove-connection with the Great Goddess: Gentle Dove, Dove-Woman, Goddess of Ancient Times; Goddess Ever Green, Priestess of Earth and Sky, Queen and Thousand-Named Goddess. As we die with Christ we come to know our Shadow Sister, and as we rise with Her we come to know Her also as Soul Sister or the One Who Makes Us Whole.

A major difference in the second volume is the occasional addition of laments. Opening prayers or collects are basically prayers of praise, and although the narrative aspect of these prayers can include the pathos of religious imagery, their short form prevents development of the grief and anger that are an important aspect of our religious experience and of the depth of our relationship with the Divine. Whereas the opening prayer carries the worshiper by means of a narrative hook, the lament sweeps us along the path of cathartic emotion to recognize at a deep level how we have been wounded and how it is that we may, in Christ/a, move to wholeness.

How These Prayers May Be Used

These prayers were written to be used in worship services where the people have been prepared to understand issues in feminist theology and wish to explore female imagery in their own worship. They are also suitable for other uses such as in worship at retreats, private devotionals and meditation, study groups, and women's groups of various kinds. It is my hope that as these images of the feminine Divine are experienced, many new images will come to mind for those traveling along the road of their quest to know Womangod. May She bless you as you continue your journey.

The Season of Advent

WOMANGOD AS PREGNANT MOTHER:
WARMING CREATION INTO BEING

I N ADVENT we are a part of nature in sense, instinct, and feeling. Our Mother is the Ocean, the Water in the womb, the Wisdom in which we lie immersed and affected more deeply than we can know. The atmosphere of Advent is pregnant with the unknown future.

In the Womb of the Divine we are connected to the Center of the Earth. We are embraced and protected. Like the chrysalis that is encased in its cocoon, we are full of potential blessings. Yet in the human womb our knowledge of love is partial and fragmented. We absorb the wounds of our mothers and the collective memory of the oppression of our grandmothers. As our mothers have had to deny their own female nature in order to survive in a patriarchal culture, we learn even before birth to deny the value of our own femaleness,[10] and we experience rejection at a depth we cannot fathom, a rejection that impairs us even before we gain consciousness. This wounding, which some might call a form of "original sin," is the wounding carried by our parents and imprinted upon our bodies and souls before we see the light of day.

In Advent we are like Inanna, Queen of Heaven and Earth, before she is moved to quest beyond the celestial sphere of patriarchy, before she is aware of a need to move beyond

what is now into the realm of human possibility. Movement
to birth, like the movement to the Last Day, is fraught with
anxiety, potential trauma; we are carried by One greater than
ourselves to a destiny of which we can know nothing. Divine
purpose carries us and brings to birth in us an awareness of
the call of redemption into which we have the privilege of
entering.

General Prayers

WOMAN DRAWING WATER

- "Joyfully you will draw water from the springs of salvation."
  (Isaiah 12:3, NJB)

    One Who Has Risen from the Sea,
    You find the oasis that has eluded us
    and draw forth for us your gift of life.
    The generosity in your smile
    and the strength of your arm offer us hope.
    Let us share the cup that You drink:
    that, nourished by your hand,
    we die and rise with You
    this day and in the Day to come.
    Source of Refreshment
    and Spring of Our Salvation,
    You are the Pool of all Wisdom. Amen.

LAMENT AT BEING ABANDONED
BY THE GREAT MOTHER

    Grandmother,
    Source of Our Being from before all time,
    You have promised to sustain us forever.

Yet even when we were in our mothers' wombs,
    You abandoned us.
Those who would oppress us turn against us
    before we see the light of day.
From sunrise to sunset
they teach us that submission is wisdom
    and claiming justice folly.
Vulnerable and alone we become prey
    for predators who would gobble us up.
Isolated and afraid, we run here and there,
    but no one will help us.
Why have You left us powerless to make our way
    in a world without mercy?
Did you create us only for shame,
so that humiliation has become our daily food?
Yet You knew us before we were conceived,
and You made us in the beauty of your own image.
In WomanChrist[11] You reach out to us
    in compassion,
and the indwelling of your Holy Spirit strengthens us
    and grounds us in overflowing love.
You heal the wounds of our hearts and bodies,
    and bind up our flagging spirits.
You call us your children, your heirs, your beloved,
    your hope.
Even when our own mothers and fathers fail us,
    You are with us.
You take us in your arms and rock us
    until we are comforted.
Old Woman, glorious is your name in all the earth!
We sing your praises forever and ever!
Amen.

Advent 1

TREE OF LIFE

- "In those days and at that time, I shall make an upright Branch grow for David, who will do what is just and upright in the country." (Jeremiah 33:15, NJB)
- "And then they will see the Son of man coming in a cloud with power and great glory...your liberation is at hand." (Luke 21:27–28, NJB)

❧   Tree of Life,
You are the Source of all things,
for your strength is like the cedar of Lebanon
whose roots stretch to the center of the earth.
With your gnarled arms gather us into your bosom.
Beneath tender leaves hide us from danger:
that, protected from those forces
    that would annihilate us,
we allow Christ to spring forth within us
and bring your Day of Justice to earth;
Great Terebinth,
Roots, Trunk, and Branches,
Triune Divinity forever! Amen.

Advent 2

MOTHER OF CREATION

- "[John the Baptist] went through the whole Jordan area proclaiming a baptism of repentance for the forgiveness of sins." (Luke 3:3, NJB)

❧   Mother of Creation,
You contained us before all time
in the ocean of your steadfast love.
Flood us with the breaking of your womb-waters:
that, carried from the safety of unconsciousness,

we enter into the light of our vulnerability;
Brooding Shadow, Child of Dawn,
Life-giving Spirit,
Womangod now and forever. Amen.

Advent 3

ECSTATIC WOMAN

To Marsha, Keri, and Celeste: Womandancers

- "Shout for joy, daughter of Zion, Israel, shout aloud! Rejoice, exult with all your heart.... Yahweh has repealed your sentence.... You have nothing more to fear." (Zephaniah 3:14–15, NJB)

☙ Ecstatic Woman,
   You sing, You shake your body with delight,
      and cry out with joy
   at the liberation of the helpless
   and the deliverance of the oppressed,
   for the disgrace of your people is taken away.
   Free us from our need to control others,
   and enable us to cast away our fear of the unknown:
   that, trusting in the sweep
   of your redemptive activity,
   we are caught up into the dance of your story,
   even to the end of Time. Amen.

Advent 4

MOTHER OF ELIZABETH AND MARY

- [Elizabeth said,] " 'Of all women you are the most blessed, and blessed is the fruit of your womb....' And Mary said, 'My soul proclaims the greatness of the Lord... because he has looked upon the humiliation of his servant.' " (Luke 1:42–55, NJB)

❧ Mother of All,
Source of courage for Elizabeth and Mary,
You gave your Child to the world,
not to be a soldier for princes,
but to bring salvation to all people.
Take from us our fear of exploitation:
that, strengthened by the depth and height
    of your love,
we grow and flourish in body, mind, and spirit.
One Who Longs for Our Healing,
Bringer of Dreams,
You are the Hope of the Universe. Amen.

The Season of Christmas
THE DIVINE MOTHER AS GIVING BIRTH TO CREATION

———— ❧ ————

C HRISTMAS is the time when we celebrate the birth of human possibility within our hearts and minds and spirits and bodies, the time when we catch sight of the potential toward which Divine Being calls us. We are Inanna, turning our faces toward consciousness, toward a desire and a willingness to grow toward wholeness.

This desire for consciousness arises in our relationship with the Divine Mother and the affirmation we experience from Her, although imperfectly, through our mothers and other nurturing persons. We experience the wonder of coming into being and the adoration in our Mother's eyes as She looks down upon us in overflowing love, as She delights in every nook and cranny of our bodies, our perfection and our imperfections, the smell of us, the feel of us. There is nothing about us that She does not love, and at our first cry She hurries to fill us with the sustaining milk of her Spirit.

Christmas is the time when we place before this All-loving Mother the inadequacies of our own capacity to love, our failures as mothers and fathers, as brothers and sisters, and as friends. It is the time when we remember our humanness but always in the light of our knowledge of the Womb-love of the Divine Mother, whose breast is ever ready to sustain us in our need. At Christmas we celebrate our humanness, which was made holy in the coming of Christ into the space of human limits of body and mind and emotion and spirit. We rejoice in our humanness, and we rejoice that Christ is ever One-with-us, growing in the well-nourished Child-within-us, giving us health and joy, wonder and passion, and bringing us to wholeness.

In creation there is the cosmic breaking of the divine water, the agony and ecstasy of giving birth, the tearing and the blood, and the afterbirth, which in primitive times was consumed. Birth is a death and a resurrection to new life, a foretaste of the Passion.

In the sense that Womangod is continually in the process of giving birth to New Creation, we carry the wonder of creative process throughout the Church Year.

General Prayers

FRIEND OF THE COSMOS

> Friend of the Cosmos,
> through your Divine Child
> You enter the soil of virgin earth.
> Let us hold You fast in our souls
>   and bodies:
> that, dying with You,
> we are awakened to new life
> and work with You
> to bring the Universe into fullness.
> Immanent One, Incarnate Child,
> You are the Bringer of Peace. Amen.

LIFE-GIVING CHALICE

> Holy Chalice,
> in the birth of the Christ Child

You poured out for us your life-blood,
and opened a way for the salvation
of the nations.
Stain us with your sacrificial goodness:
that, knowing the love from which
You created us,
we put our trust in You
for the redemption of the world.
Birth-giving Mother,
Promise of Redemption,
You are the Bringer of Eternal Joy.
Amen.

LAMENT ON THE ENSLAVEMENT
OF OUR BIRTH-GIVING POWERS

Goddess of Sun and Moon and Stars,
You made us as we are,
in your own image,
and connect our inner rhythm
to the ebb and tide of your womb-waters,
the sea.
How then could You allow our bodies
to become prisons that determine our destinies
and encage our souls?
You have allowed the rich red blood
that once told us we were your own
to become the indelible sign of our inferiority,
a curse that makes us unclean in the sight
of others.
Our very beauty and warmth endanger us
as moment by moment we steal through the jungle
of human greed;
we are objects and not persons,

abandoned by our mothers and fathers
    and even by our selves.
Once women of nobility and power and wisdom,
You made us vessels of the brutality of men.
Our strengths fled,
and our brains were numbed with fear.
We called to You,
but You no longer answered us
    or danced by our sides.
They call us stupid
and sneer at our tears.
They value us not for our selves
but for the look and feel of our bodies
and for the comfort we give to them.
What happened to your love for us?
Why have You left us for centuries
    to the devices and demands
of those who wield power over us?
Yet in the Christ Child You bring a light
    into our darkness,
and open a path for us toward dignity
    and freedom.
Though our efforts to escape oppression
    are impeded by difficulties and setbacks,
You sustain us through the wilderness
    of our own confusion
and give us once more the pride
    that was taken from us.
You strengthen us so that we can stand up
    to our oppressors.
You enlighten us with the knowledge
that we give birth with You
not only through our bodies
but in our hearts and minds.

You call us to vocations
that far exceed "biological destiny."

Teach us not to be humble
but to walk with humility in the light
of your mercies.
Help us to know the value of love,
not only for others but for ourselves,
and bring us at last to the Great Birthing
of humankind
into the Land that has no end,
even your Shalom.
Earth-wisdom,
Great Creatress,
You are the Giver of Freedom
now and forever. Amen.

Christmas Eve

DIVINE MIDWIFE

- "The people who walked in darkness have seen a great light.
  ... They rejoice before you as with joy at the harvest....
  For the yoke of their burden ... you have broken...." (Isaiah
  9:2b–4a, NRSV)
- "For the grace of God has appeared, bringing salvation to all."
  (Titus 2:11, NRSV)

ᔰ Divine Midwife,
    as You oversee the birth of the Universe,
    You wrap the outcast ones
    in the cloth of your steadfast love;
    and the sign of your coming peace
    is justice longed for, felt, and done.
    Empower us to set aside greed and comfort:
    that, turning from the ways we oppress others,

we discover our oneness with You and all humanity;
through Jesus Christ we pray. Amen.

Christmas Day

GODDESS AS WEAVER

- "All things came into being through [Christ the Word]." (John 1:1–4, NRSV)

- "... the earth ... and the heavens are the work of your hands; they will perish, but you remain; they will all wear out like clothing; like a cloak you will roll them up, and like clothing they will be changed. But you are the same, and your years will never end." (Hebrews 1:10–12, NRSV)

   Weaver of the cloak of night,
   we are the stars You knit
   into the one fine cloth.
   Continue your creative work in us:
   that when this planet's time is spent,
   heaven and earth be joined in one,
   and all creation share in your Glory.
   Ebb and Tide,
   You rock the cradle of the sleeping Child,
   and bring to birth all humanity. Amen.

SOPHIA

- "And the Word became flesh and lived among us...." (John 1:14a, NRSV)

- In Judeo-Christian tradition Wisdom (translated from Hebrew into Greek as *logos,* or "Word") has been seen as the feminine principle in divine creative activity. Through Wisdom (Sophia) the hidden design for the redemption of the world is revealed.

   Sophia Our Goddess,
   You unveil your plan of love
     for the universe

and work within creation
to bring about your purpose.
Give us the wisdom to understand
that your justice exceeds human justice,
and your love is of a quality
we only begin to discern:
that, trusting in your birth-giving powers,
we celebrate the coming
of your peace on earth;
Grandmother, Mother, and Child,
One Divinity for All Times. Amen.

Christmas 1

MOTHER WISDOM

- "[Jesus'] mother treasured all these things in her heart." (Luke 2:51, NRSV)
- "Let the peace of Christ rule in your hearts.... Let the Word of Christ dwell in you richly." (Colossians 3:15–16, NRSV)

👄 Mother Wisdom,
as You once danced in Miriam
beside the Red Sea,
You move within us to bring peace
to the peoples of the earth.
Treasure in your heart every nuance
of generosity and compassion
which springs from your Word within us:
that, knowing your trust in us,
we respond with love for You and all people;
Searcher for the Lost,
Questing One,
Flow of Love,
Womangod One-in-Three. Amen.

Christmas 2

Prayers suitable for this day:

- "Sophia Our Goddess" or "Weaver of the Cloak of Night": see Christmas Day, p. 42.
- "Mother Wisdom": see Christmas 1, p. 43.
- "Luminous Star": see Feast of the Epiphany, p. 46.

The Season of Epiphany
THE DIVINE MOTHER AS NURTURING
HUMANITY INTO MATURITY

As CHRISTMAS is symbolized by the candle in the darkness, this image is carried into Epiphany in the magi's star followed in the nighttime. This star is our nascent consciousness seeking out our Soul-mate, the One who will in every way bring us into wholeness and a joy beyond comprehension. We are Inanna making the decision to journey by night in search of Wisdom.

This star is the Mother whose kindness draws us into community with other people. The light of this star gives us motherly Wisdom, that brings into our experience deep and abiding love — love that issues in feelings of self-worth and confidence in a world which will both affirm and alienate us in our life's journey. This Great Mother, whose ancient symbol was the dove, opens to us a new understanding of baptism: the Mother claims us as Her own forever, promising to sustain, challenge, and enable us for ministry and sending us into the world as messengers of Her love.

In Epiphany the Feminine Divine is Spiritwoman running in bare feet across this garden earth to embrace all creatures. She frees us from whatever prevents us from living passionate and whole lives. We experience the enigma of the eternal Goddess whom we know in ways we cannot describe and whom we long to know more fully.

Feast of the Epiphany

LUMINOUS STAR

- "After his birth astrologers from the east arrived... asking,
  'Where is the new-born king of the Jews? We observed the
  rising of his star and... have come to pay him homage."
  (Matthew 2:1–2, REB)

> Luminous Star,
> as You led the magi
> from wisdom to Wisdom,
> You draw us into the presence
>   of the living Christ,
> and make the night
> of our souls beautiful.
> Shine on the fragile fabric
>   of our being:
> that, transformed
> by the light of your love,
> we share with others
> the joy of your healing touch;
> Queen of Heaven,
> Divine Child,
> Illuminating Spirit. Amen.

LAMENT AT THE LOSS OF THE TRADITION OF WISE WOMEN

> Ancient One,
> from the earliest times You taught us
>   about Yourself
> through the creativity and warmth
>   of our own bodies.
> The circle of your goodness through which we passed
>   month by month
> told us the pattern of your ways
> and promised us renewal of life even after death.

In all things we were at peace with You
and one another.
But You turned against us
and brought your goodness to an end!
You allowed our bodies to be violated and
degraded!
You let hordes sweep across our lands
to devour the peoples who had worshiped You
faithfully for generations,
to take by violence our power and our knowledge
of self-worth!
They twisted the very stories through which we had
remembered You;
they made the wisdom of your serpent
the source of evil,[12]
and they vanquished the dove of your soaring
to the single act of carrying an olive branch.
How we longed for You, but You were far away!
How we cried out for You, when they told us You
were no more than wooden statues or metal idols!
Yet You persisted in the wisdom of Deborah
as she sat under the palm tree.
You hid in the Cloud of the Shekinah,
Moses' Beloved and the Beloved of the children
of Israel in exile.[13]
You hovered over us as Wisdom seeking
her dear friends,
and returned as Dove-Woman in the baptism
of your Holy Child.[14]
You surfaced once more in the Syrophoenician
woman
who challenged Jesus' perception of your mercy.[15]
You spoke to our hearts and minds in the sayings
of Jesus,

and You worked in our anger wherever the Church
    acted against your wisdom,
relegating us to places of shame and humiliation.
And now, in these latter times,
You emerge in Glory to redeem all
    who are oppressed,
and to raise to life those who have perished!
Breath of Life, Holy Sophia,
we adore You forever and ever!
Amen.

First Sunday after Epiphany
(The Baptism of the Lord)

DOVE-WOMAN, GODDESS OF ANCIENT TIMES

- " ... and the Holy Spirit descended upon [Jesus] in bodily form like a dove. And a voice came from heaven, 'You are my ... Beloved.' " (Luke 3:22, NRSV)

    Dove-Woman,
    Goddess of Ancient Times,
    You descend in beauty
    and cause the mists of your Spirit
    to rise up in our hearts.
    By the power of your ecstatic presence,
    mark us as your own forever:
    that, made one with You in baptism,
    we are strengthened to minister in your name
    to all who long for your redemption.
    Queen of Heaven and Earth,
    the soft coo of your singing sustains us forever.
    Amen.

Second Sunday after Epiphany

ONE WHO SEEKS OUR GROWTH

- At the wedding in Cana of Galilee: "When the wine gave out, the mother of Jesus said to him, 'They have no wine.' And Jesus said to her, 'Woman, what concern is that to you and to me?'" (John 2:3–4, NRSV)

≈ Pushy Woman,*
You could keep us for yourself,
forever innocent and uncontaminated,
but your watchful eyes,
sharp as the owl's with wisdom,
see beyond our beauty
to our capacity to care for one another.
Nudge us out of the cocoons of our infancy:
that, tumbled into the realities of this life,
we seek justice and compassion for all people;
Elder-woman, Maturing Daughter,
Laughing-dancing Ones. Amen.

Third Sunday after Epiphany

SPIRITWOMAN

- "Jesus, filled with the power of the Spirit, returned to Galilee. ... 'The Spirit of the Lord is upon me, because he has anointed me to bring good news to the poor.'" (Luke 4:14, 18, NRSV)

≈ Spiritwoman,
You run in bare feet
through the jungles of human society
to bring freedom to all those
who suffer and are oppressed.

---

*"Pushy Woman" is said tongue in cheek, playing on the way assertive women are often perceived. If preferred, use "One Who Seeks Our Growth."

Make us the voice
that heralds your coming,
and the hands and feet
that carry out your purpose in the world:
that, restored to equality
in relationship with one another,
all people celebrate with joy
the coming of Shalom;
Heartbeat of the World,
Divine Earthling,
Morning-glory that climbs a moonbeam
to the stars. Amen.

Fourth Sunday after Epiphany

GRANDMOTHER OF THE WIDOW OF ZAREPHATH

- " '... there were many widows in Israel in the time of Elijah, when ... there was a severe famine over all the land; yet Elijah was sent to none of them except to a widow at Zarephath in Sidon....' When they heard this, all in the synagogue were filled with rage." (Luke 4:25–28, NRSV)

❧   Grandmother of the Widow of Zarephath,
in your wisdom You chose a gentile woman
to provide shelter for the prophet Elijah,
and blessed her with an unending supply
    of your grace.
Remind us that your steadfast love
is meant for all nations:
that, not hoarding your mercies,
we devote our lives to the spreading
of your gospel in word and in deed;
Defender of Women and Children,
Friend and Advocate of the Lost,
Bringer of Salvation. Amen.

Fifth Sunday after Epiphany

WOMAN OF THE DEEP WATERS OF OUR SOULS

- "[Jesus] said to Simon, 'Put out into the deep water and let down your nets....' When they had done this, they caught so many fish that their nets were beginning to break." (Luke 5:4, 6, NRSV)

    Woman of the Deep Waters of Our Souls,
You call us to cast our nets into your depths,
where is hidden more treasure than we can
     ask or imagine.
Open to us your promise of new life:
that, alerted to the abundance of your gifts,
we turn from the scarcity
of our own imaginations and follow You;
Compassionate Womb,
Sailor-woman,
Shore of Heart's Delight. Amen.

Sixth Sunday after Epiphany

GODDESS EVER GREEN

- "They shall be like a tree planted by water, sending out its roots by the stream. It shall not fear when heat comes, and its leaves shall stay green; in the year of drought it is not anxious, and it does not cease to bear fruit." (Jeremiah 17:8, NRSV)
- "But in fact Christ has been raised from the dead, the first-fruits of those who have died." (1 Corinthians 15:20, NRSV)

    Goddess Ever Green,
wintry winds cannot take away
the intensity of your color,
nor freezing temperatures
dry the flow of your sap.

Give us your tenacity to stand strong
in the midst of adversity:
that, warmed by the fires of life
deep within your belly,
we give shelter to those who are the lost
and outcast ones;
Tree of Eternal Life, Vulnerable Sapling,
Terebinth of Love. Amen.

Seventh Sunday after Epiphany

WOMANGOD WHO LIGHTS THE PATHS OF DARKNESS

- "Love your enemies, do good to those who hate you...pray for those who abuse you...for [God] is kind to the... wicked." (Luke 6:27–28, 35, NRSV)

- "So [at David's bidding] Tamar took the cakes she had made, and brought them into the chamber to Amnon her brother. ...When King David heard of [Amnon's rape of Tamar], he became very angry, but he would not punish his son Amnon, because he loved him." (2 Samuel 13:10b, 21, NRSV)

☙ Womangod Who Lights the Paths of Our Darkness,
You hold up your lamp of truth
to the deeds of those who abuse others.
The brilliance of your love
calls the wayward to responsibility
and restores dignity to those who suffer.
Energize us with the luminosity
of your goodness:
that, leaving acquiescence behind,
we find the courage to stand for justice
for the sake of all humanity;
Lover of Truth, One Who Confronts Evil,
Spirit Who Spins Gold from the Dross
of the Universe. Amen.

TAMAR'S LAMENT

❧ Great Mother,
Birth-giver of the Universe,
in my distress I cried out to You,
but You did not answer.
You sealed your ears against my terror
    and my pain.
You left me alone in my despair
    to be violated and degraded
and thrown out the door like so much garbage.
As the wolves attack the rabbit,
tear it limb from limb and devour it,
my spirit was assaulted.
My future was taken from me,
and there was no past to which I could return.
Those who should have protected me
betrayed and debased me.
By the design of my brother
and the collusion of my father
I was deceived and violated.
What is the wail of a woman's grief to men?
What is her life but to be a plaything,
a pawn in a game of cat-and-mouse,
no person,
eventually even to herself!
There is no place where a woman can be safe,
not even in her own house
nor with her own family.
Wherever we walk — the streets of our
    villages or cities,
the sacred paths of your forests
    and mountains —
we are in danger.

At the faintest sound along our way,
or the tremble of a shadow,
we start with fear,
we peer over our shoulders,
and prepare to die.
By what degree of hatred
have You turned your back on us?
Why have You stripped us of our ancient power
and brought us to shame and self-loathing?
Do not forget us! Turn back to us in mercy!
Weep with us in the tears of our mothers
    and sisters and aunts!
Hold us in their embrace,
in the gentleness of their hands stroking our hair,
in the softness of their words of consolation,
searching the recesses of our hearts for pain.
Hear us, Great Mother!
Turn our shame to anger, and our anger to action
in behalf of our sisters and all who are abused!
Turn our fear to indignation, and our hurt to
    courage!
For You are our WomanWisdom,
Who brings us to birth into new life and hope.
You are the Storm Who tears down oppressive
    structures.
You are WomanChrist,
Sophia, Who flows within us forever
and brings us to the one Safe Place
in the Land of your Shalom. Amen.

DIVINE POTTER

- "...you do not sow the body that is to be, but a bare seed, perhaps of wheat or of some other grain. But God gives it a body as he has chosen."(1 Corinthians 15:37, NRSV)

❧ Divine Potter,
You have chosen the clay of human existence
from which to bring forth things of beauty and
strength.
Help us to value our human bodies
and to care for the bodies of others:
that, reverencing You in us and all creation,
we open to your Spirit nestling within us;
Wise Creatress,
One-Who-Enters-into-Our-Flesh,
Dancing Spirit. Amen.

Eighth Sunday after Epiphany

SEER OF THE END OF TIME

- "Why do you see the speck in your neighbor's eye, but do not
notice the log in your own eye?" (Luke 6:41, NRSV)

❧ Seer of the End of Time,
You call us to turn
from the distortions of our nearsightedness
to discern your plan for all creation.
Permeate the blindness of our hearts
with the illumination of your vision of Shalom:
that, no longer judging others,
we seek with them
to bring all peoples to know You;
Grandmother Who Seeks for the Lost Children,[16]
Sight to Behold,
Eye of Love. Amen.

The Season of Lent
WOMANGOD AS SUPPORTIVE MOTHER:
OPENING THE DOOR TO OUR SHADOW SISTER

—— ❧ ——

BEFORE WHOLENESS is possible, descent is necessary. In the myth of Inanna, she must descend through the seven gates, leaving part of her clothing behind until at the end she enters naked into the presence of her shadow Self, Ereshkigal. In Christian myth Jesus moves from Galilee, where he is applauded, to Jerusalem, where he is crucified. Each of us at some time in our lives — normally adolescence — move through a kind of descent to discover who we truly are and where it is we are called to go in our life's journey.

There is a certain crisis that emerges around puberty. It is when we catch the first glimmer of the dark side of life. We had imagined, despite all the evidence to the contrary, that life is good and that the future is without doubt a time when we will find happiness. At the moment we glimpse and first begin to comprehend the pathos of life, we enter the wilderness. As children, when we met evil and hatred and rejection, we fled into the arms of our parents for comfort and reassurance. As adolescents we become aware of parental weakness and limits, and we seek an Other to sustain us as we discern evil rampant across the planet. We also reach out to our peers, who see things the way we see them. We find idols — movie stars, singers, or other public figures — people who are manifestations of the Divine Soul-mate drawing us along the path of self-discovery. They become images of heroines and heroes who move through the wilderness time with seeming courage and competence — we imagine they know what they are doing. Yet there is a real danger as we follow in their wake that we may lose our way and become stranded in the wilderness, because these personas are only fragments of the whole. Or we may attach ourselves to an image that enables us to skirt the wilderness altogether. Then we will fail to learn the secrets of our inner chaos and creativity, our anger and capacity for destructiveness and the ways in which we sabotage our own lives, our greed and our callousness toward the needs of others, and all of the potential for either evil or good that is a part of our humanness.

We will fail to reach the Promised Land, possible only through the wilderness of the chaotic self. So in Lent we welcome the Shadow Sister as the One Who enables us to know ourselves, the One Who pilots us through troubled waters, and the One Who brings us to know the Divine. She is the One Who at Eastertide emerges as Soul Sister, the One Who Knows Us inside and out and frees us from the bondage of our wilderness selves to become our whole, not partial, Self. She is the Forgiving Sister who accepts us as we are and does not despise. She values and transforms the darkness of our hearts, and leads us into the Passion of Christ toward Easter.

Ash Wednesday

SECRET TREASURE

- "But when you give alms, do not let your left hand know what your right hand is doing, so that your alms may be done in secret; and your Father who sees in secret will reward you." (Matthew 6:3–4, NRSV)

❧ Secret Treasure,
the opulence of your love
sustains where all else fails.
Lavish on us the riches
of your steadfast mercy:
that, unlocking the chambers
    of our hearts
which resist your influence,
we are filled with compassion
and brought to maturity
in partnership with You.
Storehouse of Goodness,
Prize of Value,
You are the Pandora's Box
    that brings us to life. Amen.

Lent 1

BIRTH-GIVING MOTHER

- "Jesus, full of the Holy Spirit, returned from the Jordan and was led by the Spirit in the wilderness, where for forty days he was tempted by the devil." (Luke 4:1–2, NRSV)
- Forty days represents the period of gestation.[17]

❧ Birth-giving Mother,
in this Lenten season
You take us into the Womb of your Self
for the space of forty days
and nurture us with your life's blood.
Form us anew in your own image:
that, dying to the distortions of our past,
we enter with joy into your New Creation;
Great Ancestress,

Child of Love,
Spirit Who Binds Us and Lets Us Go. Amen.

Lent 2

CHRISTA MOST SORROWFUL

- "Jerusalem, Jerusalem, the city that kills the prophets and stones those who are sent to it! How often have I desired to gather your children together as a hen gathers her brood under her wings, and you were not willing!" (Luke 13:34, NRSV)

🙢 Christa Most Sorrowful,
as with tears You surrender
to the powers of this world,
You long to gather us
under the shadow of your wings
and save us from the consequences
of our own foolishness.
Open our hearts to the wonder
of your compassion:
that, setting aside our defenses,
we are transformed by your grace
to live out our lives in love
for all the world;
in the name of Jesus our Mother,[18]
the Incarnate and Risen One. Amen.

See also "Mother Hen," The Feast of Epiphany, *Seasons of the Feminine Divine*, Cycle B (Volume 1), p. 57.

Lent 3

KINDHEARTED GARDENER

- "[The gardener] replied, 'Sir, let [the barren fig tree] alone for one more year, until I dig around it and put manure on it. If it

bears fruit next year, well and good; but if not, you can cut it
down.' " (Luke 13:8–9, NRSV)

~   Kindhearted Gardener,
    through your compassion
    for Sarah, Rebekah, and Rachel
        in their childlessness,
    You showed your faithfulness
        to all people,
    and promise to meet each of us
    at the point of our own barrenness.
    By your leniency give us the time
        to sprout and grow:
    that, as true daughters and sons,
    we give birth to love, hope, and joy
        among all peoples,
    to the Glory of your Name.
    Planter and Nurturer,
    You are both Blossomer and Harvester,
    One Divinity for all times and seasons.
    Amen.

Lent 4

WOMANGOD WHOSE LOVE KNOWS NO BOUNDS

- "But the father said to his slaves, 'Quickly, bring out a robe —
  the best one — and put it on him; put a ring on his finger and
  sandals on his feet. And get the fatted calf and kill it, and let
  us eat and celebrate; for this son of mine was dead and is alive
  again; he was lost and is found!' And they began to celebrate."
  (Luke 15:22–24, NRSV)

- Because the mercy shown by the father in this parable is like
  the womb-love of a mother who forgives all, the use of a father
  image gives us an androgynous picture of the Divine.

❧   Womangod Whose Love Knows No Bounds,
       You reclaim those parts of our minds
            and spirits
       that waste your gifts,
       and where we are self-righteous,
       You appeal to our better selves.
       Give us repentant hearts:
       that, accepting the depth
            of your forgiveness,
       we be healed of fragmentation
       and embody your compassion
            throughout the world.
       Grandmother, You draw us into One
            with You forever. Amen.

Lent 5

INVENTOR OF THE NEW CREATION

- "I am about to do a new thing;...do you not perceive it?"
  (Isaiah 43:19, NRSV)

- "Do nothing from selfish ambition or conceit, but in humility regard others as better than yourselves. Let each of you look not to your own interests, but to the interests of others."
  (Philippians 2:3–4, NRSV)

❧   Inventor of the New Creation,
       You have designed the universe
       so that each creature may receive
            all that we need,
       until we are full of your goodness.
       Spill out from your Glory love that never ends:
       that, made whole in your image,
       we are enabled to reach out to others
            in your Name.

One Who Tenderly Fashions All Things,
Stirring of Divine Wisdom,
You are Womangod forever. Amen.

WOMAN CRUCIFIED

- *Alternative Prayer* for Lent 5 based on Philippians 2:5–6:
  "Let the same mind be in you that was in Christ Jesus, who
  though he was in the form of God, did not regard equality
  with God as something to be exploited, but emptied himself,
  taking the form of a slave, being born in human likeness"
  (NRSV). See Eleventh Sunday in Ordinary Time, p. 98.

LAMENT OVER THE SUPPRESSION OF WOMEN
THROUGH CHURCH DOCTRINE

Liberating Goddess,
when in ancient times oppression overtook us,
locking us into a system that devalued and demeaned
    us for many years,[19]
You heard our cries and came to us
in the person of Jesus and in his stories and sayings.
Jesus broke the protocols of his day and associated
    openly with women.
He healed the brokenness of women's bodies and
    spirits
and spoke out against those who exploited the weak
    and the vulnerable ones.
Jesus called women to leave their traditional roles
    and follow him as disciples,
inviting them into a life of spirit and intellect.
He modeled compassion for widows, prostitutes,
    and people who were victimized.
Raising Jairus's daughter from the dead,
he offered women the hope of new life
    in the kinship of heaven.[20]

Yet after a time You turned your face from us
and allowed our fathers and brothers to betray us.
You blinded their eyes to your beauty in us,
so that they forgot our connection to You,
　　Mother of All.
They wrote out scriptures to curtail the freedom
of our ministries in the Church.
They held councils and devised doctrines
that branded us as inferior
and controlled our thoughts and actions.
Women who persisted in their independence of action
　　and thought
were enslaved, excommunicated, or martyred.
Impotent, You let them force us into docility,
while they themselves were violent and aggressive.
How could You abandon us?
How could You allow the light of our joy to be
　　turned into the shadow of our sorrow?
Yet even in the dark night of the soul
You reach out to us.
You draw us into the comfort of your bosom.
You speak to us in our sisters and brothers who know
　　your liberating power,
and encourage us with new visions of hope.
Open our hearts to the renewal of your presence
　　within us.
Reassure us that You walk beside us each step
　　of the way:
that, trusting in your mercy, we look with joy
　　to your coming Glory.
Glorious Woman Who lives in all times and seasons,
　　we praise your holy Name.
Amen.

PASSIONATE GODDESS

- "Mary took a pound of costly perfume made of pure nard, anointed Jesus' feet, and wiped them with her hair. The house was filled with the fragrance of the perfume. . . . Jesus said, 'Leave her alone. She bought it so that she might keep it for the day of my burial. You always have the poor with you, but you do not always have me.'" (John 12:3, 7–8, NRSV)

℘ Passionate Goddess,
in Mary of Bethany You show us
that love is costly, even unto death.
Enable us, like Mary,
to devote all of our being
to the love of Christ:
that, giving up our concern
for lesser things,
we be filled with the perfume
of your life-giving Spirit;
Weeping Woman,
Vulnerable One,
Sweet Odor of Joy. Amen.

Holy Week

WOMAN DYING AS THE RELINQUISHING
OF CONTROL OVER OTHERS:
LOVE AS CHOICE FOR HUMAN FREEDOM

I N HOLY Week we are led by our Shadow Sister into the crisis of meeting the deepest darkness of our souls. This darkness has vast potential for evil — or for good. It is our capacity for evil that assaults us and overwhelms us. We have the choice, as in Gethsemane, for succumbing to our capacity for evil, or for grasping the darkness within us as the chaos of creative energy for good. We welcome desire but turn from greed. We welcome anger but turn from destruction. We welcome sorrow but turn from self-pity. We submit all that would turn us from our true Self, from our Soul Sister, to the nails of consciousness that tame the undisciplined energy that has pushed us hither and yon in the wilderness journey. Only having suffered the nails of crucifixion do we come to the brink of the wholeness promised in Easter. The crucifixion, like the rape of Persephone, or Inanna nailed to the wall by Ereshkigal, brings us to consciousness — both to the consciousness of the depth of our oppression, and to the consciousness of our potential wholeness. Out of the experience of crucifixion, we discover our common humanity with other people and the emergence of a compassion of which we did not know ourselves capable. Our Shadow Sister guides us

through this labyrinth; as Shadow She is also the Promise of
Soul Sister.

As we move through this wilderness, we also experience
Goddess as Grief-stricken Mother, the One who fears for us
and mourns for us in our pain, the One who longs to give
us new birth into a new land where pain and suffering are
no more, the One who although helpless to stop our journey
still gives us and becomes for us the Bread for the journey, the
One who watches and waits with us in this time of dying, and
the One who promises life beyond the grave. In these Holy
Week prayers the presence of the Mother is seen as embodied
in the sorrows of Mary.

General Prayer

LAMENT ON THE SUFFERING OF CHILDREN

    ❧   Mother Jesus,
        You Who wept over the children of Jerusalem,
        and cried out that You longed to draw them
            under the protection of your wings,
        where are your tears now for the little ones
            who suffer?
        Now, as then, you allow them to die slow deaths
            of starvation,
        their bodies distended,
        their thin cries piercing the hearts of their mothers
            and fathers.
        Without clean water they become ill and die.
        You let them be mutilated in war,
        and physically and sexually abused the world over!
        Children grow up in the midst of violence and greed;
        yet You do nothing to save them.
        Surrounded by affluence children live in poverty,
        their mothers cast off and barely scraping by.

Is there nothing more You can do than to gather
    them to your breast at the End of Time?
You who could not save yourself on the cross,
can you not save even the infants?
Do You make us responsible for what You will
    not do?
Do You leave it all to us in our weakness
    and our self-centeredness
and our hardhearted ability to turn away
    from the pain of others?
Yet it is your anger that wells up in our own hearts,
and digs deep at the pits of our stomachs.
It is your cry that comes out of us
and shakes the mountains and trees with its agony.
It is You who give us vast resources
so that we may share them with those in need.
Awaken our awareness of your passion within us!
Teach us to use your gifts not for ourselves
but to redeem the sick, the lost, and the suffering!
Give us the courage to be willing to do with less,
and to demand more from those in positions
    of power.
Help us to take stands when our governments
fund wars to protect the interests of the rich
    at the expense of the poor.
Let us not rest until every child in every place
has enough to eat, dignity, self-respect,
and a knowledge of the infinity of your devotion.
For You, Womb of All, are the Compassion within us,
    longing to be freed;
You are the Courage of Jesus longing to be found;
and You are the flow of Love that overcomes
    all obstacles:
Divine Goddess One-in-Three forever. Amen.

Passion Sunday

GRIEF-STRICKEN MOTHER

Sequence of the Sorrows of Mary, 5:
"The Crucifixion and Death of Jesus"

- "There they crucified [Jesus]....Standing near the cross of Jesus were his mother, and his mother's sister, Mary the wife of Clopas, and Mary Magdalene." (John 19:18a, 25, NRSV)

> Grief-stricken Mother,
> as your Divine Child,
> perfect as a seamless garment,
> was snatched from your arms
> to be crucified,
> your heart was torn in two.
> Open to us the knowledge
> that You grieve as much for each
> of your children:
> that, astonished by the depth
> of your love for us,
> we pour out our lives
> as libations to the glory of your Name;
> Birth-giver of All,
> Compassionate One,
> Spirit of Justice. Amen.

WEEPING WOMAN

- "A great number of the people followed [Jesus], and among them were women who were beating their breasts and wailing for him. But Jesus turned to them and said, 'Daughters of Jerusalem, do not weep for me, but weep for yourselves and for your children. For the days are surely coming when they will say, 'Blessed are the barren, and the wombs that never bore, and the breasts that never nursed.' " (Luke 23:27–29, NRSV)

❧ Woman Who Weeps for the Ones Condemned,
as your children are shot senselessly in the streets
and ravaged in wars and famines,
You send us as lambs into the midst of wolves
to be the agents of your transforming love.
Teach us to use our grief and anger at the slaughter
of innocents
to enter with you into the labor pains
of the Universe:
that, dying with You, we rise to serve You
for all eternity;
Wailing Woman Who Beats her Breasts, Barren One,
Spirit Who Brings New Life out of sorrow. Amen.

See also "Provider of the Journey-Bread" (Luke 22:14–23),
Maundy Thursday, p. 71.

Monday in Holy Week

MOTHER GENTLE AS A TURTLEDOVE

Sequence of the Sorrows of Mary, 1:
"The Prophecy of Simeon"

• "Then Simeon blessed them and said to [Jesus'] mother
Mary ... 'and a sword will pierce your own soul too.'" (Luke
2:34–35, NRSV)

❧ Mother Gentle as a Turtledove,
your heart is pierced
by the suffering of your children,
and your hope for their happiness
dashed by evil rampant in this world.
Reach out in compassion
to every one who would turn to You:
that, redeemed by your perfect love,

we join with You to bind up the wounds
   of humanity;
Creatress of All,
Redemptress of the Lost,
Sustainer of the Universe. Amen.

Tuesday in Holy Week

GODDESS OF THE SHADOWS

Sequence of the Sorrows of Mary, 2:
"The Flight into Egypt"

- "Then Joseph got up, took the child and his mother by night,
  and went to Egypt.... Then was fulfilled what had been spo-
  ken through the prophet Jeremiah: 'A voice was heard in
  Ramah, wailing and loud lamentation, Rachel weeping for
  her children; she refused to be consoled, because they are no
  more.'" (Matthew 2:14, 17–18, NRSV)

  Goddess of the Shadows,
     as Mary and Joseph took the Divine Child
     and fled by night to Egypt,
  You, too, would gather us up
  into the safety of your dream of peace.
  Give us the courage to face the deaths
     that await us:
  that, standing firmly for the justice
  to which You call us,
  we enter into the activity
  of your redemption throughout the world;
  Mother of Visions,
  Child of Promise,
  Spirit of Liberation. Amen.

Wednesday in Holy Week

MOTHER WISDOM

Sequence of the Sorrows of Mary, 3:
"The Loss of Jesus for Three Days"

See "Mother Wisdom," prayer for Christmas 1, p. 43.

Maundy Thursday

PROVIDER OF THE JOURNEY-BREAD

- "Then came the day of Unleavened Bread, on which the Passover lamb had to be sacrificed. So Jesus sent Peter and John,
saying, 'Go and prepare the Passover meal for us that we may
eat it.'" (Luke 22:7–8, NRSV)

🙠 Provider of the Journey-Bread,
You call us to travel with You.
On this your darkest night,
give us the courage and faith to stay awake:
that we watch and pray with You
for the first gleam of dawn
on the Day of Resurrection;
Maker of the Universe,
Incarnate One, Spirit of Peace,
Womangod Three-in-One. Amen.

ONE WHO WASHES THE FEET
OF THE SERVING WOMAN

- "Having loved his own who were in the world, [Jesus] loved
them to the end.... [He] got up,... took off his outer robe,
and tied a towel around himself. Then he poured water into a
basin and began to wash the disciples' feet." (John 13:1, 4–5,
NRSV)
- In taking the role of the lowest servant who washed the feet of
the family and guests, Jesus dignified the role of this servant.
It is likely that the lowest servant in the house was female.

Although not recorded in scripture, it is conceivable that Jesus, in taking the lowest role from her, would have been willing to wash her feet.

෨   One Who Washes the Feet
    of the Old Serving Woman,
    You give value and dignity
        to those who are scorned
    for their low positions in this world.
    As You have received us,
    teach us to welcome the poor
        and the unskilled:
    that, setting aside our roles of power,
    we enter into relationship with You
        and all humanity.
    Old Washer-woman,
    Scrubber of the nooks and crannies
        of our hearts and minds,
    You purify the earth with your mercy.
    Amen.

Good Friday

AWAKENER

- "Awake, awake! Clothe yourself in strength, Zion. Put on your finest clothes, Jerusalem.... The chains have fallen from your neck, captive daughter of Jerusalem! ... so many nations will be astonished and kings will stay tight-lipped before him; seeing what had never been told them, learning what they had not heard before. (Isaiah 52:1, 15, NJB)

- "Incarnating, you have redeemed me; dying, you have awakened me. Now you have brought all your work to fullness — in virgin nature you found pasture, in virgin nature you assumed flesh" (Hildegard of Bingen).[21]

   ❧   Maker of Heaven and Earth,
in virgin nature You assumed flesh
   and found pasture,
redeeming the people of your hand.
Through your death awaken us to compassion:
that, manifesting your love for the world,
we become co-creators with You
in the unfolding of the divine-human story;
Creatress, Christ, and loving Spirit,
One Divinity for all eternity. Amen.

MOTHER BEREFT

Sequence of the Sorrows of Mary, 4:
"The Ascent to Calvary"

- "So they took Jesus; and carrying the cross by himself, he went out to what is called The Place of the Skull, which in Hebrew is called Golgotha." (John 19:16b–17, NRSV)

   ❧   Mother Bereft,
You watched your Divine Child
walk away from You, alone,
to carry on his own shoulders
the burden of the sin of the world,
and You could not prevent his death.
Stand with us when we, too,
longing to mother your children,
find ourselves unable to help:
that, weeping with You,
our tears be transformed
into comfort and hope;
Mother of Eve,
Mother of Christ,
Mother of Us All. Amen.

Saturday in Holy Week

MOTHER OF THE VICTIMS OF OPPRESSION

Sequence of the Sorrows of Mary, 6 and 7:
"Jesus Taken Down from the Cross" and
"Jesus Laid in the Tomb"

- "The women who had come with [Jesus] from Galilee followed, and they saw the tomb and how his body was laid. Then they returned, and prepared spices and ointments." (Luke 23:55–56, NRSV)

- "Now there was a garden in the place where [Jesus] was crucified, and in the garden there was a new tomb in which no one had ever been laid. And so, because it was the Jewish day of Preparation, and the tomb was nearby, [Joseph of Arimathaea and Nicodemus] laid Jesus there." (John 19:41, NRSV)

❧   Mother of the Victims of Oppression,
       although your children have been taken
       from the garden of this world,
       they can never leave the garden of your love.
       Cause to spring up within us
       the blossoms of your undying mercy:
       that, committing our lives to the pursuit
            of justice,
       we plant with You the seeds of Life Eternal;
       Weeping Woman,
       Crucified and Risen One,
       Spirit Who Breathes into Us the Hope of Shalom.
       Amen.

The Season of Easter

WOMANGOD AS SOUL SISTER:
ACCEPTING FREEDOM AND SELF-DETERMINATION

W E DO NOT emerge fully intact from the Lenten encounter. We emerge as ones wounded, Christ crucified, Inanna nailed to the wall, and knowing the woundedness of others. In the time between Good Friday and Easter
we have moved through the deepest crisis of human existence. As we make this passage, knowing our capacity for
evil, we renounce evil. In the renouncing of evil, we are freed
into the possibility of integrating the chaos within us and
moving toward wholeness. The Feminine Divine has become
our Bridge from fragmentation to wholeness. We emerge
from this Passover cleansed from self-hatred and full of love
for ourselves and all creation. It is at this moment, this season
of spring in the human-divine encounter, that we are ready to
give ourselves in love to the Divine and to other people.

The Easter experience is full of excitement and elation
at getting free from the cocoon of adolescence and moving into New Creation. Inanna is released from death. She
breathes in air, stretches, feels her body come to life, receives
nourishment, and moves toward freedom.

In Easter all creation comes alive with vibrancy and color
that overwhelms us with a sense of Her presence and fills
us with joy: joy that Womangod is alive, around us, above
us, and below us. Life, which was once dreamlike when we

moved as though in some somnolent state, opens up for us
the abundance of intense joy that has surrounded us all of
our lives but whose touch we have not felt until this time.
As well, Life takes on a sacramental character that we have
not before discerned: there is a benevolence from Goddess
that we have known in a kind of symbiotic way, but now
receive at the hand of our Priestess as we ourselves become
priestesses at the altar of life.

General Prayer

FIERY BLOSSOM

陀 Fiery Blossom,
    You run rampant across the meadow
        of human consciousness
    and enrich our world with the colors
        of your love.
    Catch our breaths into awe at your splendor:
    that, inspired by your beauty,
    we cultivate gardens of joy
    where all will live in justice and peace;
    Flower of Passion,
    Bleeding Heart,
    Fireweed that flames in the night
        of our souls. Amen.

The Great Vigil of Easter

LAMENT OVER THE LOSS OF WOMEN'S STORIES
IN SALVATION HISTORY

陀 Great Goddess,
    known from ancient times as Creatress and Savior,
    as in the darkness of this night we recite the story
        of your salvation of the world,

of creation and fall,
of Israel redeemed and lost and redeemed again,
and of your coming in Jesus Sophia to reconcile
  humankind once more to You,
we cry out to You at the absence
  of women's names
among those to be remembered tonight.
Tonight, Sarah, who laughed aloud in delight
  at the promise of a child in her old age,
  is forgotten.
Where are Rebekah, Rachel, Leah or the other
  matriarchs?
Did Miriam not dance with her sisters beside
  the Red Sea?
Did Deborah not sit beneath the palm tree
  and prophesy?
Where is Ruth, who modeled a commitment
  like that of Abraham and Sarah as they traveled
  to a foreign land?
Where is Esther, who, like Moses, saved her people?
We grieve at the omission of the names
  of our foremothers!
We weep over the women whose roles were crucial
  to the unfolding of your story of salvation,
but whose names have been lost to us and
  to our sisters and daughters forever!
Deprived of their names and stories,
we came to believe that women were of little
  importance to You.
We expected nothing from You—nothing at all.
Where did we disappoint You, that You turned
  away from us?
What evil did we do, or what good did we fail
  to remember,

that You looked the other way when those in power
   excluded us from your story?
We wail like children deserted by their mothers!
We flood the earth with the tears of our mourning!
We rage, we shout, we shriek in indignation
   at the way that You abandoned us.
The length of your absence overwhelms
   and demoralizes us.
Nevertheless, like Miriam secreted among
   the bulrushes,
You have followed us in our dark journey.
Hidden in the clouds above us, You encircled us
   in the mist of your Love,
and your bell-like voice echoed between
   the mountains and the valleys of our sojourn.[22]
Yahweh's hidden spouse, You accompanied
   us through deserts and high places.[23]
Although we did not know it, You whispered to us
   your words of wisdom.
Many times You checked our vital signs.
When we despised ourselves, You wept with us.
When we suffered, You shared our pain,
and yes, when we discovered joy,
   You celebrated with us!
We welcome You into our midst, Sister of our souls,
holy is your Name!
On this night of nights,
we sing praises to You Who never forget your own,
and give thanks to You for all your daughters
   past and present, known and unknown,
who have embodied You in every age.
We worship You, Goddess Three-in-One:
Cherubim, Hokmah, and Shekinah,
now and forever. Amen.

For prayers reflecting women's experience in Holy History, which might be included in the sequence of scripture passages to be read at the Easter Vigil, see:

- "Mother of Creation," Advent 2, p. 34

- "Goddess of Deborah," Twenty-Ninth Sunday in Ordinary Time, p. 124

- "Mother Wisdom," Christmas 1, p. 43

- "Grandmother of the Widow of Zarephath," Fourth Sunday after Epiphany, p. 50

- "Woman of Honest Wealth (Wisdom)," Twenty-Fifth Sunday in Ordinary Time, p. 116

- "Mother of All," Advent 4, p. 36

- "Dove-Woman, Goddess of Ancient Times," First Sunday after Epiphany, p. 48

- "Passionate Goddess," Lent 5, p. 64

- "Christa Most Sorrowful," Lent 2, p. 59

- "Woman Crucified," Eleventh Sunday in Ordinary Time, p. 98

- "Friend of Joanna and the Two Marys," Easter Day, p. 80

See also in *Seasons of the Feminine Divine,* volume 1, Cycle B:

- "Mother of Sarah and All Humanity," Lent 2, p. 69

- "Courage of Esther," Proper 26 after Pentecost, p. 113

- "The Goddess in the Women Who Did Not Flee,"
  Good Friday, p. 81

- "Women at the Burial of Jesus," Holy Saturday, p. 82

- "Mary Magdalene, First Apostle," Easter Day, p. 86

Easter Day

- " ... on the first day of the week, at early dawn, [Mary Magdalene, Joanna, Mary the mother of James, and the other women
  with them] came to the tomb, taking the spices that they
  had prepared.... 'Why do you look for the living among the
  dead? He is not here, but has risen....' Then they remembered
  [Jesus'] words." (Luke 24:1, 5, 8, NRSV)

FRIEND OF JOANNA AND THE TWO MARYS

❧   Friend of Joanna and the Two Marys,
      it was first to women that You revealed
      the miracle of your power over death
      and sent abroad the message of hope
         for all who are in need.
      Wipe away the tears of our doubts,
         fears, and sorrows:
      that, receiving the good news
         of Christ risen,
      we hurry to proclaim with joy
      that death is not the end
      but the beginning of life abundant;
      Blessed Womangod,
      You are the Redemptress of the Distressed,
      and the Bridge Who draws us
      across the turbulence of life. Amen.

PRIESTESS WHO OPENS HER HAND TO THE NEEDY

- In the ancient goddess religions it was the role of the priestesses to prepare the bodies of the dead for burial. This was not
merely a functional role; it was a sacred activity that enabled
these women to look death in the eye, thereby developing the
ability to face death with courage and to help their people to
face deaths in their own experience.[24]

❧　Priestess Who Opens Her Hand to the Needy,
　　You bring healing ointments
　　to the places in our lives where death lurks,
　　and create a bridge for us to leave behind
　　　　our fragmented selves.
　　Allure us with the sweet smell of your spices:
　　that, our senses opening to the fragrance
　　　　of your love,
　　we enter into the Home that You prepare for us,
　　where want and suffering have ceased,
　　and the needs of all people are met
　　　　with compassion and equity.
　　Woman of Wisdom, Emerging Maiden,
　　and Blessed Ruah, You flow forever,
　　world without end. Alleluia! Amen.

See also "Mary Magdalene, First Apostle," Easter Day, *Seasons of the Feminine Divine*, Cycle B (Volume 1), p. 86, with
reference to John 20:1–18.

Second Sunday of Easter

INFINITE LOVE

- "'I am the Alpha and the Omega,' says the Lord God, who is
and who was and who is to come, the Almighty." (Revelation
1:8, NRSV)

❧ Infinite Love,
    the alpha and omega of your ardor
    free us from bondage to human limits,
    and make us priestesses at the altar of life.
    Open to us the joy of vitality in Christ:
    that, coming to new birth in the dawning
        of your Shalom,
    we serve You in all that we do and are.
    One who is, was, and is to come,
    we worship You forever.
    Amen.

BATTERED WOMAN

• " ... but [Thomas] answered, 'Unless I can see the holes that
the nails made in [Jesus'] hands ..., and unless I can put my
hand into his side, I refuse to believe.' " (John 20:25, NJB)

❧ Battered Woman,
    in your body You carry the affliction
        of humanity,
    and day by day You taste our mortality.
    Let us touch the gash across your face,
    the broken bones, the myriad bruises
        You sustain unceasingly:
    that, given courage by the knowledge
        of your suffering within us,
    we work to end all violence against women.
    Source of Well-being,
    Wounded Healer[25]
    You are the Sister Who Reaches Out
        with Compassion.
    Amen.

One Who Prowls the Jungle of Life:
A Lament for Ones Abused

- "For I will be like a lion to Ephraim, and like a young lion to the house of Judah. I myself will tear and go away; I will carry off, and no one shall rescue. I will return again to my place until they acknowledge their guilt and seek my face. In their distress they will beg my favor." (Hosea 5:14–15, NRSV)

One Who Prowls the Jungle of Life,
You describe yourself as a lion
who tears the body of its own child.
You intimidate us through violence
and coerce us through fear,
and by your actions You justify
the use of force in human relationships.
Because of You women and children
   have suffered abuse,
and whole peoples have been misused.
How can You say that You are a God of love?
And how can You command us to love
   our neighbors as ourselves?
Show us that You are compassionate
   and not full of hatred!
Convince us that the name "Lion"
   is not your own,
but the invention of the prophet
out of the crudity of his own emotions!
For You are the One who comes to us
   with tenderness.
Your anger is clean and fair
and never seeks power over us.
Your hand is always open
and never closes to us.
Patiently You wait for us to come to You.

Your care for us is unconditional
    and never fails.
As your Spirit of compassion grows
    and blossoms across the cosmos,
turn the hearts of the peoples
    to justice and truth:
that all persons are given dignity
    and respect,
and enabled to become fully human
    in your image;
for You, Heavenly Dove,
are the One who persuades the Lion
to lie down in peace with the Lamb
in your eternal garden of love.
Amen.

Third Sunday of Easter

QUEEN OF THE UNIVERSE

*To my dear friends in the parish of St. Margaret's,
Edmonton, Alberta*

- The image in this prayer is based on Queen Margaret of Scotland, who, though of lofty position, was known for going through the land giving money and other gifts to the poor.

- " . . . I heard the voice of many angels surrounding the throne and the living creatures and the elders; they numbered myriads of myriads and thousands of thousands, singing with full voice, 'Worthy is the Lamb. . . . To the one seated on the throne and to the Lamb be blessing and honor and glory and might forever and ever!' " (Revelation 5:11–14, NRSV)

- "And the one seated there looks like jasper and carnelian, and around the throne is a rainbow that looks like an emerald." (Revelation 4:3, NRSV)

❧ Queen of the Universe,
myriad creatures in heaven and on earth
and in the vastness of space beyond
bless your name and sing praises
to the Christ, the Holy One.
Rise from your throne
to embrace the poor and the lame,
the sick and the afflicted:
that, experiencing your graciousness,
all are drawn into your rainbow Circle;
Glorious and Risen One,
Shekinah-with-us forever. Amen.

Fourth Sunday of Easter

EMERGENT WISDOM

- "...there was a great multitude that no one could count, from every nation, from all tribes and peoples and languages, standing before the throne...singing,...'Blessing and glory and wisdom and thanksgiving and honor and power and might be to our God forever and ever!'" (Revelation 7:9–12, NRSV)

❧ Emergent Wisdom,
You have opened the door to redemption,
and all the people of the Universe
will praise your Name and worship You.
Bring us across the threshold
of your living grace:
that, leaving behind doubt and despair,
we rejoice with You and all creation
at your coming Glory;
Lady Sophia, Living Word,
Consummating Spirit. Amen.

Fifth Sunday of Easter

- "Little children, I shall be with you only a little longer...
  where I am going, you cannot come... love one another... just
  as I have loved you." (John 15:33–34, NJB)

MOTHER WHO LETS US GO

✺   Mother Who Lets Us Go,
       You have sustained us with the abundance
          of your love
       and brought us to maturity.
       Send us into the world with your blessing:
       that, living in mutuality with one another,
       we carry out your mission to bring Earth
       and all humanity into health and wholeness.
       One Who Loved Us from before all Time,
       You are Christa-within-us,
       the Spirit Who Draws Us into the eternal sphere
          of your peace. Amen.

CHILD WITHIN US

✺   Child within Us,
       You fill us with awe at the beauty of creation
       and open us to a world lush with possibility.
       Teach us to value our vulnerability,
       and show us how to trust one another:
       that, letting go of the facades we draw about us,
       we enter into the kinship of your love
       and live in mutuality with all people.
       Christa Most Holy, You bring this Universe
          to health and wholeness. Amen.

SOUL SISTER

- "...he will wipe every tear from their eyes. Death will be no more; mourning and crying and pain will be no more, for the first things have passed away." (Revelation 21:4, NRSV)

☙ Soul Sister,
You transform all that is evil
and fill us with the good that is You alone.
Wipe away every tear from the cheeks
    of your sisters and brothers,
kiss away the pain that has turned us
    from one another,
and enfold us in the tenderness of your embrace:
that, leaving behind suffering and loss,
we enter the house that You prepare for us;
Mother of Comfort,
Homemaker,
Flow of Love. Amen.

Sixth Sunday of Easter

SISTER SHEKINAH

- "But the Advocate, the Holy Spirit, whom the Father will send in my name, will teach you everything." (John 14:26, NRSV)
- "And in the spirit he carried me away to a great, high mountain and showed me the holy city Jerusalem coming down out of heaven from God. It has the glory of God and a radiance like a very rare jewel, like jasper, clear as crystal." (Revelation 21:10–11, NRSV)
- "...and the city did not need the sun or the moon for light, since it was lit by the radiant glory of God." (Revelation 21:23, NJB)

☙ Sister Shekinah,
You draw us into your divine place of safety,
where earth and heaven are one,

and light reflects the Glory of your presence.
Illumine the paths we walk in search of You:
that, celebrating the goodness of your Being,
we enter into the joy of unity with You
    and one another;
Goddess of the Hearth of the Universe,
Sacred Bridge, Spiritwoman,
Triune Divinity forever. Amen.

Ascension Day

GENTLE QUEEN

- "...and [Jesus] said to them, 'Thus it is written, that the
  Messiah is to suffer and to rise from the dead on the third
  day, and that repentance and forgiveness of sins is to be proclaimed in his name to all nations, beginning from Jerusalem.
  You are witnesses of these things....' Then...lifting up his
  hands, he blessed them...and was carried up into heaven."
  (Luke 24:46–48, NRSV)

- "When he had said this, as they were watching, he was lifted
  up, and a cloud took him out of their sight." (Acts 1:9, NRSV)

ॐ   Gentle Queen,
     through the death and resurrection
         of your Divine Child,
     You bring earth and heaven into unity
         with You,
     the Dawning of human possibility.
     Receive us into the warmth
         of your maternal bosom:
     that, nourished by your steadfast love,
     we witness to your work of redemption
     and await your coming in Glory;
     Welcoming Mother,
     Crucified and Risen One,

Spirit Who Draws All into Wholeness,
Triune Goddess forever. Amen.

See also "One Who Greens the Earth with Your Glory: A
Lament on the Rape of the Earth," Eighteenth Sunday in
Ordinary Time, p. 104.

Seventh Sunday of Easter

QUILTER OF THE NEW CREATION

For Jackie, Womanquilter

- " 'See, I am coming soon....I am the Alpha and the Omega,
  the first and the last, the beginning and the end.' Blessed are
  those who wash their robes, so that they will have the right to
  the tree of life and may enter the city by the gates." (Revelation
  22:12–14, NRSV)

> Quilter of the Galaxies,
> from our fragmented bodies and souls
> You gather remnants
> to stitch into the pattern of the Universe.
> Piece together the scraps
> of our lost dreams and aspirations:
> that, transformed by the magic of your skill,
> You bring into being the New Creation;
> Maker of All That Is,
> Thread That Draws Us through the Needle's Eye,
> Fabric of Our Hope and Joy. Amen.

Prayers for Pentecost and After
GODDESS AS MATURE WOMAN

As CHILDREN we were dependent on others, particularly adults, for love. Although we could be loving, we could not be in an equal relationship with another person because our resources of love were too fragile, too unformed. In Easter we have moved from self-love to Love and into the exhilaration of New Being and mutuality. Easter, as a kind of coming of age, is the point in time when we cross over from needing to be loved to being able to love. In Pentecost this mutuality is brought to fruition. We discover how Love forms the very core of our being. We are full of Love and Love is consummated within us. In that moment we become a part of Love itself, enthralled, radiant, and eternal. As our Soul Sister, Womangod makes her home in us; She is Woman-Christ within us. Love is internalized and cannot be taken from us. From this time forward we participate in redemptive Love in every aspect of our being as we enable one another to live in redemptive ways. WomanChrist becomes our Divine Enabling One and lives redemptively in and through us.

In the images of maturity Womangod moves more deeply into compassion. Inanna, ascended through the seven gates, having regained her full regalia of royal splendor, is restored to her throne. Once more Queen of Heaven and Earth, she is not the same as she was before her descent. Like Jesus she has tasted death, experienced hell, and confronted evil. Wounded

herself, Womangod takes on the wounds of others. She is
present in women who are assaulted. She is present in women
of color who suffer racism as well as gender discrimination.
She is also present in every woman who suffers.

In Pentecost we celebrate the activity of women in the
Church and lament the ways the Church has caused women
to suffer — the doctrines that have split apart body and
soul, dividing us within ourselves and against ourselves and
one another. We lament the abuse of women and the loss
of women's leadership roles in the early Church. The Divine Feminine as Wise Woman emerges in images of women
pursuing justice: Womangod Who speaks her mind, Who un-
locks hearts, Who warms and strengthens us with Her Glory,
Angry Old Woman, Trickster Who subverts the old order,
Revolutionary, and Fire of Justice.

Finally, the Feminine Divine calls us into the autumn of our
earthly life. She leads us once more toward the Womb of the
Goddess from which we came, so that we may prepare for
our final birth into the Land of Shalom where all people are
One in the radiance of her Love forever.

General Prayers

SOURCE OF WISDOM

      Source of Wisdom,
        You are the Secret Room
        in the house of our souls
        where a wealth of understanding
        is stored.
        Open our hearts and minds
        to these treasures:
        that, enriched by your grace,
        we carry the abundance of your love
        to the world;

Sophia, Bride, and Girl-Child,
One Goddess forever. Amen.

THOUSAND-NAMED GODDESS

❧   Thousand-named Goddess,
You come to us in the many guises
of our mothers, sisters, aunts, and daughters.
Help us to know You in our relationships
     with one another:
that, as holy women and men,
we live out your mission
to herald your redemption of the world;
One who will be whoever we truly need,
Goddess Three-in-One. Amen.

PRIESTESS OF EARTH AND SKY

❧   Priestess of Earth and Sky,
You decorate the blue-vaulted heavens
with sun and moon and stars,
and You fill the land with good things.
Breathe your vitality
into the activity of our day,
and illumine our contemplation
of You by night:
that the cosmos sing with the joy
of your wholeness,
and all become One in You;
Creatress, Nurturer,
and One Who Brings Us Home. Amen.

DIVINE OLD WOMAN

❧   Divine Old Woman,
the frailty of your bones,

the whiteness of your hair,
and your rippled skin
witness to the long-suffering love
You have given to this creation.
Give us the strength
to accept our mortality,
the things we have achieved
and the things left undone:
that, prepared to return
to the Time before Time,
we rest in You, Ocean of Eternal Bliss,
for You are the Wise and Holy One,
together with the Mother and Child,
One Goddess forever more. Amen.

Prayers for Pentecost and the Sundays in Ordinary Time from May 8 to July 2

Goddess as Woman
Moving into Adult Responsibility

The Day of Pentecost

WOMANSPIRIT

- "I shall pour out my Spirit on all humanity. Your sons and daughters shall prophesy, your old people shall dream dreams, and your young people see visions." (Joel 3:1, NJB)
- "All of them were filled with the Holy Spirit and began to speak in other languages, as the Spirit gave them ability." (Acts 2:4, NRSV)

✿ Womanspirit,
　　You rejoice when the gifts You have given us
　　come to life and take form and embody your beauty
　　　　to the world.

You laugh aloud with delight and bless us
    for who we are, as we are,
and celebrate with us the joy of creative adventure.
Give us the courage to trust your intelligence,
    which rises within us,
and the confidence to bring into being
    from our hearts and souls new creation:
that, becoming partners with You,
we give birth to the new world
    into which You lead us;
for You are the Old Woman who spins out
    the Song of our lives,
the Dance of Wisdom. Amen.

GENTLE DOVE

- "Peace I leave with you; my peace I give to you. I do not give to you as the world gives. Do not let your hearts be troubled, and do not let them be afraid." (John 14:27, NRSV)

- " . . . I will pour out my Spirit upon all flesh." (Acts 2:17, NRSV)

  Gentle Dove,
    rising before us in the morning dew,
    You ruffle your feathers
    to shake off lingering mists of night.
    With your soft voice call us to come to You:
    that, permeated by your love,
    all creation be healed of its wounds
    and made one with You forever;
    Wings that surround and protect,
    Breast that gives warmth,
    Phoenix, ascending from the ruins
    of human sin to redeem the world. Amen.

See also "Lament at the Loss of the Tradition of Wise Women," prayer for the Feast of the Epiphany, p. 46.

Trinity Sunday

WOMANGOD THREE-IN-ONE

- "The Lord created me [Wisdom] at the beginning of his work, the first of his acts of long ago. Ages ago I was set up, at the first, before the beginning of the earth.... When he established the heavens, I was there, when he drew a circle on the face of the deep...I was beside him, like a master worker; and I was daily his delight." (Proverbs 8:22–23, 27, 30, NRSV)

- "When the Spirit of truth comes, he will guide you into all the truth." (John 16:13, NRSV)

❧ Womangod Three-in-One,
You circle about us
in the dance of life overflowing,
promising wholeness if we but follow You.
Catch us up in the swirl of your playfulness:
that, filled with the joy of your loving-kindness,
we enter with You through the gates of Shalom.
Mother, Sister, and Child,
You surround us with your love forever! Amen.

Sixth Sunday in Ordinary Time (May 8–14)

HEALER OF BRUISED MINDS AND BODIES

- "[The people] had come to hear [Jesus] and to be healed of their diseases; and those who were troubled with unclean spirits were cured.... Blessed are you who weep now, for you will laugh." (Luke 6:18, 21b, NRSV)

❧ Healer of Bruised Minds and Bodies,
at your touch we are made well
and empowered to reach out to others
in your Name.
Give us the strength to stand against
violence and greed:
that, encouraged by your justice,

we hasten toward that day
when all will leap for joy
in your Resurrection Land;
we pray in the name of Christa,
our Heart and our Passion. Amen.

Seventh Sunday in Ordinary Time (May 15–21)

SEED OF LIFE

• "So it is with the resurrection of the dead. What is sown is perishable, what is raised is imperishable." (1 Corinthians 15:42, NRSV)

Seed of Life,
implanted within the dark spaces
of our selves,
You enable us to die to all
that turns us from You and one another.
Put forth within us the shoots
of your love and wisdom:
that, opening to You, Who are our Source,
we grow in depth of compassion;
Wise Woman, Midwife, and Divine Child,
Triune Divinity for all Seasons.
Amen.

Eighth Sunday in Ordinary Time (May 22–28)

PLAYFUL GODDESS

• "Listen, I will tell you a mystery! We will not all die, but we will all be changed, in a moment, in the twinkling of an eye, at the last trumpet. For the trumpet will sound, and the dead will be raised imperishable, and we will be changed." (1 Corinthians 15:51–52, NRSV)

∞ Playful Goddess,
    with the wink of your eye
    You beckon us into friendship with You,
    and tease us with the promise of new possibility.
    Open to us the realization
    that death cannot destroy:
    that, reassured by the warmth of your smile,
    we enter into the transformation of your love;
    Laugh of Sarah,
    Dancing Wisdom,
    Shout of Joy. Amen.

Ninth Sunday in Ordinary Time (May 29–June 4)

LOVER OF ALL

- "[Solomon said], 'O Lord, God of Israel, there is no God like you in heaven above or on earth beneath, keeping covenant and steadfast love for your servants who walk before you with all their heart.'" (1 Kings 8:23, NRSV)

∞ Lover of All,
    your dwelling place is in the heart
        of creation
    from which flows the fullness
        of your steadfast mercy.
    Kiss the wounds of us your beloved:
    that, healed by the gentleness of your touch,
    we embrace the world with acts of compassion;
    Woman of Generosity,
    Vulnerable Supplicant,
    Desire that Binds All into One. Amen.

See also "Healer of Bruised Minds and Bodies," Sixth Sunday in Ordinary Time (after Pentecost), p. 95.

- "[The Jewish elders said] '[The centurion] is worthy of having you [heal his servant], for he loves our people, and it is he who built our synagogue for us....' When those who had been sent returned to the house, they found the slave in good condition." (Luke 7:4–5, NRSV)

Tenth Sunday in Ordinary Time (June 5–11)

ONE WHO HAS LOVED US FROM BEFORE ALL TIME

- "But when God, who had set me apart before I was born and called me through his grace, was pleased to reveal his Son to me, so that I might proclaim him among the Gentiles, I did not confer with any human being... but I went away at once into Arabia." (Galatians 1:15–16, NRSV)

🙿   One Who Has Loved Us from Before All Time,
You have brought us into being
and nurture us to maturity.
Reveal to us the purpose
of our existence:
that, dreaming the dream You dream,
we claim the path that You open before us;
Benevolent Mother,
One Who Co-journeys with Us,
Rainbow Spirit. Amen.

Eleventh Sunday in Ordinary Time (June 12–18)

WOMAN CRUCIFIED

- "I have been crucified with Christ; and it is no longer I who live, but it is Christ who lives in me. (Galatians 2:19, NRSV)

🙿   Woman Crucified,
for seeking justice
for the afflicted ones of the world,
You are insulted and abused.

Give us the courage to stand
with our sisters and brothers who are oppressed:
that, though we suffer with You,
we press on with your passion for justice;[26]
Grieving Old Woman,
Vulnerable Maiden,
Fiery Spirit, forever. Amen.

Twelfth Sunday in Ordinary Time (June 19–25)

VOICE OF JUSTICE

- "Then the word of the Lord came to him, saying, 'What are you doing here, Elijah?' He answered, 'I have been very zealous for the Lord.... I alone am left, and they are seeking my life to take it away.' Then the Lord said to him, 'Go, return on your way to the wilderness.'" (1 Kings 19:9–10, 14–15, NRSV)

- "...for in Christ Jesus you are all children of God through faith.... There is no longer Jew or Greek, there is no longer slave or free, there is no longer male and female; for all of you are one in Christ Jesus." (Galatians 3:26, 28, NRSV)

Voice of Justice,
when our hearts are sore
from the violations of our rights
and those of others,
the sound of your nearness
reassures and comforts us.
Speak to us of your steadfast love,
and strengthen us with your promise
of freedom:
that, empowered by your Wisdom,
we persevere in the work of redemption
You set before us:
Mother's Call for Her Lost Children,

Cry of the Oppressed,
Song of Hope. Amen.

Thirteenth Sunday in Ordinary Time (June 26–July 2)

WHIRLWIND SPIRIT

- "As [Elijah and Elisha] continued walking and talking, a char-
  iot of fire and horses of fire separated...them, and Elijah
  ascended in a whirlwind into heaven." (2 Kings 2:1–2, NRSV)

- "For freedom Christ has set us free....If you are led by the
  Spirit, you are not subject to the law." (Galatians 5:1, 18,
  NRSV)

ᔥ   Whirlwind Spirit,
    You spin around us the net of your breath
    and snatch us from all that would keep us
      from You.
    Liberate us with the wisdom of your gospel:
    that, caught by the passion of your coming,
    we become lovers with You of all people;
    Storm of Our Desire,
    Tempestuous One,
    Breath of Life. Amen.

Prayers for the Sundays in Ordinary Time from July 3 to August 20
Goddess as Advocate for the Marginal and Dispossessed

Fourteenth Sunday in Ordinary Time (July 3–9)

ASSAULTED GODDESS

- "See, I am sending you out like lambs into the midst of
  wolves." (Luke 10:3, NRSV)

- "And Ahab said to Naboth, 'Give me your vineyard, so that I may have it for a vegetable garden, because it is near my house...' and the scoundrels brought a charge against Naboth, in the presence of the people...[and] they took him outside the city, and stoned him to death." (1 Kings 21:2, 13, NRSV)

- "From now on, let no one make trouble for me; for I carry the marks of Jesus branded on my body." (Galatians 6:17, NRSV)

☙ Assaulted Goddess,
    as the vineyard of this earth is plundered,
    You suffer the wounds of all creation.
    Protect us from a callousness of heart
    that would overlook the ruthlessness
        of the powerful,
    and show us that our vulnerability
    is the strength that You have given us:
    that, sent as lambs into the midst of wolves,
    we are empowered for good by your love
    which contains and flows through us;
    for You are the Strength of the Afflicted,
    the One Who Endures the Evil of the World,
    and the Spirit of Mercy. Amen.

Fifteenth Sunday in Ordinary Time (July 10–16)

SISTER OF COLOR

- In the story of the Good Samaritan, Jesus shocked his listeners by making a person whom they looked down upon, a Samaritan, the hero of the story, thus challenging us through the ages on issues of racism and attitudes of exclusiveness about our religions (Luke 10:25–37).

☙ Sister of Color,
    You are the One we have not seen
    as we passed You on the street.

You are the One whose voice has gone unheard.
You are the One who more than any other
has suffered the contempt of the world.
Yet in You compassion has bloomed
bright as the fireweed upon the mountainside,
sweet as the perfume of the magnolia tree,
and as certain as the solitary beauty
    of the lotus bud.
Open our eyes to our common humanity:
that, giving up the protection of our prejudices,
we cease all divisiveness;
for You are the Angel of Mercy,
the Friend Who Pours Oil on the Wounds
    of Humanity,
and our Shekinah, Who Carries Us in her arms
    to the place of eternal safety.[27]
Amen.

Sixteenth Sunday in Ordinary Time (July 17–23)

WOMANGOD WHO SPEAKS HER MIND

- "But the Lord answered her, 'Martha, Martha, you are worried and distracted by many things; there is need of only one thing. Mary has chosen the better part, which will not be taken away from her.'" (Luke 10:41, NRSV)

🙟   Womangod Who Speaks Her Mind,
        to Mary You gave a heart of contemplation,
        but in Martha You placed a spirit of activism.[28]
    Free each of us to become who it is
            You intend us to be:
        that, giving up our slavishness
        to traditional expectations,
        we join with You in bringing into being
            your new humanity;

Serene Sister,
Assertive One,
Circle of Divine Wisdom. Amen.

Seventeenth Sunday in Ordinary Time
(July 24–July 30)

DOOR OF MANY SHAPES AND COLORS

- "Ask, and it will be given you; search, and you will find; knock, and the door will be opened for you. For everyone who asks receives, and everyone who searches finds, and for everyone who knocks, the door will be opened." (Luke 11:9–10, NRSV)

🙟   Door of Many Shapes and Colors,
      You welcome all who come to You
      and unlock the hearts of those
          who would turn away.
      Invite us to enter into the Land
          of your Glory
      where the last are first
      and the first are last:
      that, lavished with the gifts
          of your hospitality,
      we share the riches of your grace
          with all humanity;
      Mother Who Listens
          for her returning children,
      Opening One, Portal of Goodness,
      Triune Goddess now and forever.
      Amen.

Eighteenth Sunday in Ordinary Time
(July 31–August 6)

PEARL OF GREAT PRICE

- "Take care!...one's life does not consist in the abundance of possessions." (Luke 12:15, NRSV)

≈   Pearl of Great Price,
    You capture the colors of the rainbow
    as You encircle and contain us
        in the radiance of your Glory.
    Teach us the value of your justice:
    that, discerning between love and exploitation,
    we be filled with the riches of your wisdom
    and live in peace with our sisters and brothers
        in your New Creation;
    Grandmother of Jewels,
    Prism of the Human Condition,
    Teardrop that makes Heaven and Earth one. Amen

ONE WHO GREENS THE EARTH WITH YOUR GLORY:
A LAMENT ON THE RAPE OF THE EARTH

- This lament was written in response to the damage of biblical writings that promote a dualistic view of reality that has devalued women, people of color, and the earth, and in gratitude for those passages that enable us to challenge the dualism of our tradition.

- "Set your minds on things that are above, not on things that are on the earth, for you have died, and your life is hidden with Christ in God....You...will be revealed with him in glory." (Colossians 3:2, NRSV)

- "Above all, clothe yourselves with love, which binds everything together in perfect harmony." (Colossians 3:14, NRSV)

≈   One Who Greens the Earth with your Glory,
    we cry out to you at the rape of this planet,

which has torn our bodies and spirits apart
so that we are no longer whole.
How is it that those who call You by Name
devalue your very body and our own?
How is it that those who call You by Name
violate You and all vulnerable ones,
leaving the land in waste
and women and children and men of color
     desolate?
You who proclaim that to sow is to reap,
bring down upon the heads of the violators
the consequences of their actions!
Draw your circle of protection about the weak
     and those on the margins of society:
that they be fed and nurtured and strengthened
to stand against the evils that assail them.
For You, Goddess, are the transforming power
     of Love,
and in all that is, You desire wholeness.
You created this cosmos and called it good.
You lavished her with mountains and hills,
with flowers and streams and all manner of wildlife.
You entrusted her into the hands of humankind.
Leave us not to the evil of our ignorance and greed!
Turn our hearts once more to You:
that, restored to ourselves and to each other,
we live out the unity of heaven and earth
     and of body and spirit
in the world without end.
Weeping Mother who wanders the planet
     in search of her ravaged children,
Crucified One,
You are the Spirit of Our Empowerment. Amen.

Nineteenth Sunday in Ordinary Time (August 7–13)

ONE WHO COMES IN THE NIGHT

- "Blessed are those slaves whom the master finds alert when he comes; truly I tell you, he will fasten his belt and have them sit down to eat, and he will come and serve them. If he comes during the middle of the night, or near dawn, and finds them so, blessed are those slaves." (Luke 12:37–38, NRSV)

- "Now faith is the assurance of things hoped for, the conviction of things not seen.... Therefore from one person [Abraham] ... descendants were born, 'as many as the stars of heaven and as the innumerable grains of sand by the seashore.'" (Hebrews 11:1, 12, NRSV)

✍ One Who Comes in the Night,
    You hide your face in the shadows
        of the trees,
    as, with stars in your hair,
    You glide through slatted moonlight.
    Give us the discipline to be ready
        for your coming:
    that, claiming the treasure of unity with You,
    we enter into your vision of Shalom;
    Old Woman Who Sees in the Dark,
    Celebrant of Earth and Heaven,
    Spirit-waves that ripple on the sands of Time,
    Womangod Three-in-One. Amen.

Twentieth Sunday in Ordinary Time (August 14–20)

FIRE OF JUSTICE

- "I came to bring fire to the earth, and how I wish it were already kindled!...Do you think that I have come to bring peace to the earth? No, I tell you, but rather division! From now on five in one household will be divided...mother against daughter and daughter against mother, mother-in-law against her daughter-in-law and daughter-in-law against mother-in-law." (Luke 12:49–53, NRSV)

✤ Fire of Justice,
You poise to sweep the earth
with the flame of your purifying love
that divides woman from woman
   and man from man.
Inflame us with your zeal to restore
   the abused
and raise the downtrodden:
that, freed from oppressive systems,
we follow You with confidence
into your World without End
where every person is cherished
   and given dignity;
through Christ,
our Mentor and our Savior.
Amen.

Prayers for the Sundays in Ordinary Time from August 21 to October 8

Womangod as Queen of the Universe: Initiator of Female Leadership in Church and World

Twenty-First Sunday in Ordinary Time (August 21–27)

DOOR OF MANY SHAPES AND COLORS

• "Strive to enter through the narrow door; for many...will try to enter and will not be able....People will come from east and west, from north and south, and will eat in the kingdom of God. Indeed, some are last who will be first, and some are first who will be last." (Luke 13:24, 29, NRSV)

See the prayer for the Seventeenth Sunday in Ordinary Time (July 24–30), p. 103.

QUEEN OF THE UNIVERSE

- "...you have come to...Mount Zion and the city of the living God, the heavenly Jerusalem where millions of angels have gathered for the festival." (Hebrews 12:22, NJB)

See the prayer for the Third Sunday of Easter, p. 85.

VULNERABLE ONE

- In this story Jeremiah sees Babylon overrunning Judah as the instrument of divine punishment, which he believes the people deserve because of their unfaithfulness. Although Jeremiah has told the people that Babylon will conquer Judah and the neighboring nations, the prophet Hananiah predicts peace. Jeremiah responds mockingly "...in the presence of the priests and all the people.... 'May the Lord...fulfill the [optimistic] words that you have prophesied, and bring back to this place from Babylon...all the exiles.... As for the prophet who prophesies peace, when the word of that prophet comes true, then it will be known that the Lord has truly sent the prophet.'" Jeremiah, however, awaits punishment for Israel. (Jeremiah 28:5–9, NRSV)

- "And if you say in your heart, 'Why have these things come upon me?' it is for the greatness of your iniquity that your skirts are lifted up, and you are violated." (Jeremiah 13:22, NRSV) This text suggests that women are to blame for being raped because of their sinfulness, and that at least on occasion rape is an appropriate punishment for a woman who has, in someone's eyes, "sinned." In the following prayer I assume that there is never an appropriate occasion for rape or for war and that particularly women and children are victims of unwarranted violence.

❧ Vulnerable One,
despised and rejected,
your skirts are flung above your head
as they cast You down and violate
   your body and spirit.
You cry out but no one hears.
Show us how to turn shame to anger:
that, comforted and sustained
   by your suffering with us,
we are enabled to give our lives
with courage and compassion
for the cause of justice;
Weeping Woman,
Mirror of Our Oppression,
You are the Hope of Resurrection
   for all peoples. Amen.

See also "Tamar's Lament," Seventh Sunday after Epiphany, p. 53.

Twenty-Second Sunday in Ordinary Time (August 28–September 3)

GRACIOUS HOSTESS

• [Jesus said,] "When you give a luncheon or a dinner, do not invite your friends or your brothers or your relatives or rich neighbors, in case they may invite you in return, and you would be repaid. But when you give a banquet, invite the poor, the crippled, the lame, and the blind. And you will be blessed." (Luke 14:12–14 NRSV)

❧ Gracious Hostess,
You invite the lame, the poor, and the blind
into your home for a party,
and entertain them in seats of honor.

Call to us in the poverty of our spirits:
that, drawn by your generosity
into your eternal Household,
we, too, search the by-ways
for the lost and the despairing,
and draw our sisters and brothers
into the banquet of your Shalom;
Mistress of the Household,
One Who Displaces the Rich and Powerful,
Spirit Who Turns the World Upside Down.
Amen.

STRENGTH OF THE EARTH

- "...if a man is upright...and he does not...touch a woman during her periods...someone like this...will live — declares the Lord." (Ezekiel 18:5–9, NJB)

Strength of the Earth,
   your birth-giving powers
      frighten and overwhelm us,
   for You turn our worlds upside down.
Give us hearts of openness:
   that we learn to flow with your
      creative process,
   and give birth in our own lives
   to actions full of your grace;
Woman Who Unsettles in order to create,
Banished and Abandoned One,
Rhythm of the Universe.
Amen.

Twenty-Third Sunday in Ordinary Time (September 4–10)

ARCHITECT OF THE NEW CREATION

- "For which of you, intending to build a tower, does not first sit down and estimate the cost, to see whether he has enough to complete it?" (Luke 14:28, NRSV)

ॐ   Architect of the New Creation,
  out of the womb of your imagination
    You envision New Being
  and draw a picture of the redemption
    of your community of love.
  Oversee the building up of your Church:
  that, opening to the movement
    of your inventiveness,
  we become the materials
    of your New Creation;
  Planner Who sets the spheres into motion,
  Engineer of the flow of the Universe,
  Brainstorm Who streams into Eternity.
  Amen.

CLEAR-EYED GODDESS

- "Now you, mortal, say to the house of Israel, ... 'Our transgressions ... weigh upon us, and we waste away because of them; how then can we live?' Say to them, As I live, says the Lord God, 'I have no pleasure in the death of the wicked, but that the wicked turn back from their ways and live.'" (Ezekiel 33:10–11, NRSV)

ॐ   Clear-eyed Goddess,
  You have written the story
    of humankind
  in the Book of Life;
  to You there is nothing new

under the sun or moon or stars.
Give us a vision of the earth
   as You intend it to be:
that, turning from self-deception,
we commit ourselves to your reality.
Source of Truth, Justice, and Wisdom,
we praise your Name forever.
Amen.

ONE WHO INVITES US INTO MINISTRY

- "To Philemon our dear friend and co-worker, to Apphia our sister, to Archippus our fellow soldier, and to the church in your house." (Philemon 1–2, NRSV)

   One Who Invites Us into Ministry,
   You drew Apphia and her sisters
   into leadership in your Church,
   and endowed them with gifts of love,
      wisdom, and discipline.
   Strengthen the hearts of women today:
   that, responding to your call,
   we embody You in word and in deed
   in the bringing of your Shalom to earth;
   for You have created us in your image,
   full of your beauty and truth:
   Womangod, WomanChrist, and Womanspirit,
   Thousand-named Goddess now and forever.
   Amen.

LAMENT OVER THE LOSS OF WOMEN'S LEADERSHIP ROLES IN THE CHURCH

   Thousand-named Goddess,
   Who made Earth the cradle of humankind,

Who sent Sarah, Rebekah, and Rachel
    to explore new lands,
and Who came in the Risen Christ first to
    Mary Magdalene and the other women,
your Spirit flowed in the work of Priscilla, Lydia,
    and Apphia and all of the female leaders
    in the early Church.
Women traveled to all parts of the world,
evangelizing, instructing
    and baptizing the newly converted.
Women blessed the bread and wine at your
    holy meal,
were ordained deacons with the laying on of hands,
led house churches, prophesied, and became
    presbyters and bishops.
Yet You turned from us and allowed us to fall back
    into the old role of submission.
They stopped our dance of ecstasy and shut our
    mouths and made us cover our heads in shame!
They forbade us to administer the sacraments.
Hemmed in on all sides we bowed to the will of those
    stronger than we were;
we became meek and trembled before those who
    dominated us.[29]
O Jesus Sophia,
once You touched us with compassion and
    raised us up!
Why did You hide your face from us and
    leave us motherless and without sisters
    to comfort and support us?
Hear the grief we pour out before You!
Speak to us in our degradation,
and lead us out of the oppression
    of our own silence and fear.

For You are Shekinah, the One Who weeps with us
    by the waters of Babylon;[30]
You are Shaddai, whose eternal milk strengthens us
    in the midst of injustice;[31]
and You are Hokmah,[32] WomanWisdom,
    within us.
You turn our tears to laughter and our despair
    into hopefulness.
Opening the doors of monasteries to women,
    You freed us from servitude in marriage.[33]
You came to us on Spirit's wings in Hildegard
    and Julian
    and the women mystics who kept
        your memory alive.[34]
Through the gift of prophecy You revealed yourself
    in exceptional women —
Margaret Fell,[35] Mary Baker Eddy,
Aimee Semple McPherson[36] — and others;
and in these latter days You arise once more
    in Glory
in the many women who claim You as their own
    and seek to serve You in roles of leadership.
As You make your Self known to us, teach us
    to worship You in your fullness:
that, no longer fragmented but whole,
all people know themselves as created in your image
    and cherished as your own child.
Mother of All, Sophia's Breath,
You are WomanWord[37] within Us,
and we glorify your Name to the end of Time
    and forever.
Amen.

Twenty-Fourth Sunday in Ordinary Time (September 11–17)

MANAGER OF THE ESTATE OF THE COSMOS

- "Or what woman having ten silver coins, if she loses one of them, does not light a lamp, sweep the house, and search carefully until she finds it?" (Luke 15:8, NRSV)

> Manager of the Cosmos,
> You sweep the floor of clay
> in quest of the one coin
> lost from your store of wealth.
> Search out those parts of our hearts
> and minds
> which are closed to the bounty
> of your love:
> that, not wasting the resources
> You have given us,
> we become generous stewards
> of your many gifts to us;
> Cosmic Homemaker,[38]
> Seeker of the Missing,
> Wise One Who knows every name
> by heart. Amen.

See also "One Who Prowls the Jungle of Life: A Lament for Ones Abused," Second Sunday of Easter, p. 83.

- "The Lord said to Moses, 'I have seen this people, how stiff-necked they are. Now let me alone, so that my wrath may burn hot against them and I may consume them....' But Moses implored the Lord.... 'Turn from your fierce wrath...and do not bring disaster on your people.'" (Exodus 32:9–12, NRSV)

Twenty-Fifth Sunday in Ordinary Time (September 18–24)

WOMAN OF HONEST WEALTH

- "Whoever is faithful in a very little is faithful also in much; and whoever is dishonest in a very little is dishonest also in much. If then you have not been faithful with the dishonest wealth, who will entrust to you the true riches?" (Luke 16:10–11)

- "A capable wife who can find?.... She rises while it is still night and provides food for her household.... Her lamp does not go out at night.... She opens her hand to the poor.... She opens her mouth with wisdom, and the teaching of kindness is on her tongue." (Proverbs 31:10–31, NRSV)

   Woman of Honest Wealth,
    You manage your estates with vigilance,
    getting up long before daylight
       to direct the work of your servants.
    You see that your employees
       are clothed and fed,
    and give all that You do not need
       to the poor.
    Give us clarity of heart and mind:
    that, no longer hoarding your riches,
    we overcome dishonesty and greed
    and seek equity in all things for all people;
    Womangod, You are Executive, Servant,
    and Spirit of Homemaking,
    One Divinity forever. Amen.

Twenty-Sixth Sunday in Ordinary Time
(September 25–October 1)

MISTRESS OF THE STORES OF THE EARTH

- "For the love of money is a root of all kinds of evil, and in their eagerness to be rich some have wandered away from the faith and pierced themselves with many pains. But as for you ... pursue righteousness, godliness, faith, love, endurance, gentleness.... Take hold of the eternal life, to which you were called." (1 Timothy 6:10–12, NRSV)

- "You shall eat in plenty and be satisfied.... And my people shall never again be put to shame." (Joel 2:26, NRSV]

🙿   Mistress[39] of the Stores of the Earth,
the bounty of your hand is sufficient
for all the peoples of this world.
Turn our hearts from the greed
that pollutes this cosmos:
that, sharing all that we have
with our sisters and brothers in need,
we cease to assault this planet
    with our voracity,
and open the way to justice for all;
Clear-eyed Goddess,
Weeping One,
Seeker of the Lost,
Womangod Three-in-One. Amen.

Twenty-Seventh Sunday in Ordinary Time
(October 2–8)

SISTER OF LOIS AND EUNICE

- "I am reminded of your sincere faith, a faith that lived first in your grandmother Lois and your mother Eunice and now, I am sure, lives in you. For this reason I remind you to rekindle the gift of God that is within you.... For God did not give us a spirit of cowardice, but rather a spirit of power and of love and of self-discipline." (2 Timothy 1:5–7, NRSV)

- Note: Although the Roman Catholic and Episcopal lectionaries eliminate the reference to Lois and Eunice, their identity is implicit in what follows in verse 6, "for this reason...."

ᔥ   Sister of Lois and Eunice,[40]
      not through motherhood but by faith
      You call women into service with You.
      Enable us to give up silence
      and timidity that is born of fear:
      that, inspired by the trusting actions
          of our foremothers,
      we enter into full partnership with You
      in the redemption of the world;
      Ancient Grandmother,
      Wise Virgin,
      and contemporaneous Spirit,
      Womangod throughout the ages. Amen.

Prayers for the Sundays in Ordinary Time from October 9 to the Reign of Christ
The Feminine Divine as Elder-Woman

General Prayers

QUEEN OF EARTH AND HEAVEN

ᔥ   Queen of Earth and Heaven,
      your judgments of mercy and kindness
      transform the hearts of humanity,
      and remove enmity and strife
      from the face of the planet.
      Bring this cosmos into the fullness
          of your majesty:

that, permeated by the intensity
of your love,
we become living messages of your redemption
of the world.
Woman of flowing robes,
your light step along the Milky Way
stirs up the very stars
and draws your Universe into the Glory
of your Shalom! Amen, amen!

WOMANGOD WHO CALLS US TO WHOLENESS

Womangod Who Calls Us to Wholeness,
You created the heaven and the earth
and the waters below the earth,
and day by day You make all things new.
Heal the fragmentation of our hearts and souls:
that, drawn into the sphere of your compassion,
we see the vision that You see,
and seek with all our being to serve You
in the Land of your Shalom.
Blessed Mother Jesus,
You sustain us forever! Amen.

Twenty-Eighth Sunday in Ordinary Time (October 9–15)

ELDER-WOMAN

• "As [Jesus] entered the village, ten lepers approached him. Keeping their distance, they called out, saying, 'Jesus, Master, have mercy on us!' When he saw them, he said to them, 'Go and show yourselves to the priests.' And as they went, they were made clean.... [The one who turned back and thanked Jesus] was a Samaritan." (Luke 17:12–14, 16b, NRSV)

✎ Elder-woman,
from the wine of your womb-love
You create the universe
and bring healing to the sick
and rejected ones.[41]
Pour out upon us the elixir
of your divine mercy:
that, touched in the innermost parts
of ourselves,
we are restored as your beloved
to wholeness and joy;
One Whose Splendor gave birth
to the angels,[42]
Eye of Wisdom,[43] Holy Sophia,[44]
Goddess Three-in-One. Amen.

GODDESS AS WOMAN SWEEPING

- "The women of my people you drive out from their pleasant houses; from their young children you take away my glory forever. Arise and go; for this is no place to rest, because of uncleanness that destroys with a grievous destruction." (Micah 2:9–10, NRSV)

- "Do not sweep me away with sinners, nor my life with the bloodthirsty, those in whose hands are evil devices.... But as for me, I walk in... integrity; redeem me, and be gracious to me." (Psalm 26:9–11, NRSV)

- "[The ten lepers] called out, saying, 'Jesus..., have mercy on us!' When he saw them, he said to them, 'Go and show yourselves to the priests.' And as they went, they were made clean." (Luke 17:13–14, NRSV)

- Barbara Walker describes the maternal power of the Goddess as not only benevolent but realistic: power that sweeps all resistance aside like chaff.[45]

9.   Womangod,
      You sweep your floors clean
      of all that would contaminate
      the holiness of the earth, our sanctuary,
      and bring down justice like rivers
      upon those who devour the vulnerable ones
          of the world.
      Empower your Church to advocate
          for the victims of war and oppression:
      that, restored to your original blessing,[46]
      all persons glorify You in word and deed;
      Angry Old Woman,
      One Who Hears the Cries of the Needy,
      Wind That Changes the Face of the Planet.
      Amen.

Harvest Thanksgiving

MISTRESS OF THE STORES OF THE EARTH

- "For the Lord your God is bringing you into a good land,
  a land with flowing streams...waters welling up in valleys
  and hills, a land of wheat and barley, of vines and fig trees
  and pomegranates, a land of olive trees and honey, a land
  where you may eat bread without scarcity, where you will lack
  nothing." (Deuteronomy 8:7–9a, NRSV)

- "Then Jesus said to them, 'Very truly, I tell you, it was not
  Moses who gave you the bread from heaven, but it is my Father who gives you the true bread from heaven. For the bread
  of God is that which comes down from heaven and gives life to
  the world.' They said to him, 'Sir, give us this bread always.' "
  (John 6:32–33, NRSV)

See prayer for the Twenty-Sixth Sunday in Ordinary Time,
p. 117.

LAMENT AT THE ABUSE OF ELDER-WOMEN
PAST AND PRESENT

    Goddess, my Goddess,
    why have You forsaken me?
    They cast me off like an old shoe.
    When I was young and lovely,
    they gave me everything;
    I was admired and respected.
    Now that I am gray and wrinkled,
    and can no longer hold my back straight,
    no one remembers my name or cares that I exist.
    One by one the treasures
    I accumulated over the years
       of my life disappear.
    Even before I am in the casket,
    they take what I have of value.
    If I speak up for myself,
    they strike me across the face;
    they push me so that I fall
       and break my bones.
    When I offer the wisdom
    I have learned in my time,
    they scoff at me and ridicule me.
    At one time in history if I insisted
       upon the truth that I knew,
    they called me a witch
    and burned me at the stake.
    When I found the courage to face death,
    preparing for burial the bodies
       of those who had died,
    they named the straightness of my gaze
    that saw through the transience of life
       the "evil eye."

When I was left a widow,
no one took care of my needs;
day after day I had no more to eat
than a cup of tea and one piece of toast.
Men were recognized for their work
and given pensions,
but my work was called nothing;
I was left to beg in the streets
and to collect garbage in back alleys.
Do not forget me, Grandmother of Old!
Remember how I put my only coin
in the treasury of your Temple!
Remember how well I cared for my children
when they were small!
Remember how I held the grieving ones
and supplied food for the poor!
For it was from You that I learned compassion,
and from You that I have gained my strength!
All the day long I meditate
on your sustaining mercy,
and remind myself that You are my hope
and my joy.
For You are my Mother and my Sister;
You are my Lover and the Child within me.
In the night You cradle me,
and in the morning You sing songs of love
to me.
Call those who worship You to conscience,
One Who Suffers with the Needy!
Hear the cries of the forgotten ones,
and bind up all their wounds!
Blessed Goddess, Three-in-One, hear me!
Amen.

Twenty-Ninth Sunday in Ordinary Time
(October 16–22)

GODDESS OF DEBORAH

- "In that city there was a widow who kept coming to [the judge] and saying, 'Grant me justice against my opponent.'" (Luke 18:3, NRSV)

- A biblical image in contrast to the unjust judge in the passage from Luke above: "At that time Deborah, a prophetess...was judging Israel. She used to sit under the palm of Deborah between Ramah and Bethel in the hill country of Ephraim." (Judges 4:4, NRSV)

> ❧ Goddess of Deborah,
>   You hear the pleas of the distressed
>   and the perplexed,
>   and offer counsel to those in conflict.
>   Attend the cry of your people for justice,
>   and answer the prayers of those, who,
>   persistent like the widow,
>   put their trust in your promise of mercy:
>   that, reassured by your compassion,
>   we move with clarity into the blessings
>   of your eternal Shalom.
>   Wise Old Woman, Seer of Truth,
>   we praise your name forever. Amen.

All Saints' Day

WISE OLD WOMAN

- May the God of glory "give you a spirit of wisdom...so that, with the eyes of your heart enlightened, you may know what is the hope to which he has called you." (Ephesians 1:17–18, NRSV)

- "Blessed are you who are poor...who are hungry...who weep...who are hated and rejected and defamed....But woe

to you who are rich...who are full...who are laughing."
(Luke 6:20–26, NRSV)

- "Blessed are the meek...those who hunger and thirst for righteousness...the merciful...the pure in heart...the peacemakers." (Matthew 5:5–12 NRSV)

❧ Wise Old Woman,
with halting step You lead each generation
to join the caravan of your saints
in its trek through holy history.
Open our hearts to the sagacity
    of your intelligence:
that, letting go of what is false,
we enter with You into the truth
    of your redemption,
where the first are last
and the last first;
for You are Womangod,
Heart and Soul of the world without end.
Amen.

Thirtieth Sunday in Ordinary Time (October 23–29)

RASCALLY OLD WOMAN

- "The Pharisee, standing by himself, was praying thus, 'God, I thank you that I am not like other people: thieves, rogues, adulterers, or even like this tax collector.'" (Luke 18:11, NRSV)

❧ Rascally Old Woman,
You are the Trickster Who would subvert
    the old order of the world,
and by the sleight of your divine Hand
bring in the new, not as the world brings,
but as your very own.
With the shrewdness of your eye,

see through the facades
which we build to protect ourselves:
that, though our lives hang
by the single thread of your compassion,
we be transported into the grace-land
     of your humanity
and flourish in the community of Shalom
     forever;
One Who Confronts and Woos Us,
WomanWisdom forever. Amen.

DIVINE RADIANCE

- "But you, O Lord, are a shield around me, my glory, and the one who lifts up my head." (Psalm 3:3, NRSV)

- Zephaniah 3:1–9 depicts arrogance and self-sufficiency as sins. Judith Sanderson, however, suggests that pride and over-confidence are rarely women's sins; rather, women need to learn "to give up their low self-esteem and dependence,... learning a pride that will value the self as much as others and that will rely on God for empowerment to take responsibility for their own actions."[47]

Mother and Lover of All,
     we have forgotten the look of your face
and can no longer remember the touch
     of your embrace.
Yet daily You walk with the broken-hearted,[48]
and weep with us as we wander in search
of lost Jerusalem.
Awaken your Wisdom in us,
     and show us that, in You, we are all-sufficient:
that, immersed in your Radiance,
     we become lamps of your loving-kindness forever.

Elder-woman,
Sagacious One Who unites heaven and earth,
You are the Soul of the Universe.
Amen.

Thirty-First Sunday in Ordinary Time
(October 30–November 5)

CALL OF THE SYCAMORE TREE

- "[Zacchaeus] was trying to see who Jesus was, but on account of the crowd he could not, because he was short in stature. So he ran ahead and climbed a sycamore tree to see [Jesus], because he was going to pass that way." (Luke 19:3–4, NRSV)

   Call of the Sycamore Tree,
   with the rustle of your leaves
   You beckon to the shortsighted,
   and your branches give a platform
      to those who wish to see.
   Speak to the longings of our hearts
      with words of forgiveness;
   extract us from the tangled compromises
      which ensnare us:
   that, freed of the fictions
      of our successes,
   we enter the reality of your graciousness;
   Voice that rises in lost valleys,
   Seeker of those who have strayed,
   Spiritwoman Who flies with hope
      to the ends of the Earth.[49]
   Amen.

Thirty-Second Sunday in Ordinary Time (November 6–12)

REVOLUTIONARY GODDESS

- "Some Sadducees ... came to [Jesus] and asked him a question, 'Teacher, Moses wrote for us that if a man's brother dies, leaving a wife but no children, the man shall marry the widow and raise up children for his brother.'" (Luke 20:27–28, NRSV)[50]

    Revolutionary Goddess,
      out of your heart of compassion
      You hear the cries of women
      who are bound to men not out of love,
         but for survival.
      By the power of your Gospel,
      open up new patterns of living
         in community:
      that, released from the chains of poverty,
      we are restored to dignity in your image;
      Whirlwind of Justice,
      Redemptress of the Downtrodden,
      Giver of the Peace that Passes
         All Understanding. Amen

Thirty-Third Sunday in Ordinary Time (November 13–19)

TEMPESTUOUS GODDESS

- "When some were speaking about the temple ... [Jesus] said, 'As for these things that you see, the days will come when not one stone will be left upon another; all will be thrown down.... Nations will rise against nation; ... there will be great earthquakes, and in various places famines and plagues; and there will be dreadful portents and great signs from heaven.'" (Luke 21:5–6, 11, NRSV)

❧ Tempestuous Goddess,
You whirl across the earth
leaving destruction in your wake,
for, in order to raise new cities,
the old are torn down.
Give us the vision to see those parts
of our structures and traditions
that have become obsolete,
and those which beckon us to newness
and life:
that, letting go of all that brings
about death and decay,
we discover the new beginnings
to which You ever call us;
Glorious Old Woman,
One Who Enlightens the Lost,
Flowing Spirit,
ever One-in-Three. Amen.

The Last Sunday after Pentecost: The Reign of Christ

THIEF WHO COMES IN THE NIGHT

- "...if the owner of the house had known in what part of the night the thief was coming, he would have stayed awake and would not have let his house be broken into. Therefore you also must be ready, for the Son of Man is coming at an unexpected hour." (Matthew 24:43–44, NRSV)

- "...for in [Christ] all things in heaven and on earth were created, things visible and invisible, whether thrones or dominions or rulers or powers — all things have been created through him and for him...in him all things hold together. ...For in him all the fullness of God was pleased to dwell, and through him God was pleased to reconcile to himself all things...by making peace through the blood of his cross." (Colossians 1:16–20, NRSV)

- "The Pharisees then said to one another, 'You see, you can do nothing. Look, the world has gone after him!" (John 12:19, NRSV)

❧ Thief Who Comes in the Night,
You steal only those who are your own
from the ones who have usurped and distorted
your divine authority.
Cause the powers and principalities
of this earth to tumble down:
that, enabled to share with joy
the resources that You have given us,
we tend the least first,
and labor with You to meet the needs
of every creature in every place.
Secretive One,
You transform us forever,
even when we do not know your
WomanWisdom.
Amen.

A LAMENT ON THE USE OF JUDGMENT IN THE CHURCH

❧ Queen of the Universe,
You have told us that your Love is perfect.
With love You gave each of your creatures
beauty and dignity.
Yet many times You have allowed the strong
to seize the authority that is yours alone,
and to exert power over others without their
consent.
In your Name prophets and kings enforced worship
of You by military might.
In your Name they wiped out those who had
known You as the Great Mother,

so that the name Yahweh, Lord of Hosts,
struck terror, not delight, into the hearts of the
    populace.
In the Name of Jesus, who laid no hand
    on his enemies but loved them,
your Church proclaimed a gospel not of peace
    but of the sword,
justifying Roman armies to wipe out whole
    communities who knew You by another name.
In your Name leaders of the Church condoned those
who imposed their understanding of the faith
    over others,
persecuting with anathemas, excommunication,
    and martyrdom
all those who disagreed with them.
The more You allowed persons in power
    to define your love,
the more hate-filled they became,
swarming across the earth to subdue the nations
    through violence,
in the same breath speaking of your love!
Always your Church kept its power
by depicting the wrath of your vengeance
and the threat of eternal damnation.
They force us to consent to the rape of our intellects
or to risk exclusion from your family.
They strip us of dignity and coerce us with the fires
    of hell.
The compassion of your Child, the Christ,
    becomes a mockery to us.
How can You claim to be divine Love?
The word "love" becomes a terror to us,
and the source of our deepest betrayal!
Tell us that your Name has been used in vain!

Prove to us that your love has been distorted
   and misused for centuries
   by those who were corrupted by power!
Demonstrate to us the love that transforms
   rather than destroys!
Show us discipline and correction
   that is gentle and cherishing,
love that persists but never forces,
love that names but never dominates,
love that empowers but never exerts power
   over others,
love that prevents but also enables,
love that states a clear "no" but waits patiently
   for us to learn and grow,
and love that says "yes" to the deepest part
   of ourselves,
so that we want none other than You, our Beloved.
Lady of Wisdom, You love us with a love
that melts the barriers of our hearts
and opens us to a world full of wonder![51]
Blessed Mother of the Earth!
Blessed Crucified and Risen One!
Blessed Flow of Devotion that embraces
   all creation!
Blessed are You, Triune Goddess, forever and ever!
Amen.

WOMANGOD WHO CALLS US HOME

- This image of grandmother was inspired by my memory of
  my own step-grandmother and the garden around the house in
  Greenwood, Texas, where I frequently played with my siblings
  and cousins.

∾ Grandmother of All,
   as we romp in the garden of this world,
   the lamp of day flickers, dusk descends,
   and You call us to come Home to supper.
   Full of the joys of the moment,
   we resist your call and cling to the last shaft
       of sunlight,
   scampering with our friends between beds
   of marigolds and day-lilies, lantanas and sweet pea,
   through the shadowed arch of the honeysuckle vine,
   circling the house where You prepare the family meal.
   Open the door of the dwelling You have prepared
       for us:
   that, smelling the fragrance of the bread that You
       bake,
   of steamed apples, and of wine,
   we run with delight into the warmth of your love
   and claim the wholeness You have promised us
       from before all Time.
   Wise Woman,
   Lover of Creation,
   You are the Song that draws the Universe
   into completion in the world without end,
   alleluia! Amen.

Notes

—— ❧ ——

1. For an alternative view that the male role in procreation was understood in ancient matriarchal societies and was seen as complementary, see Elinor W. Gadon, *The Once and Future Goddess* (San Francisco: Harper & Row, 1989), 8–14.

2. This name was drawn from the title of a book by Miriam Therese Winter, *WomanWisdom* (New York: Crossroad, 1991).

3. Jean Baker Miller, *Toward a New Psychology of Women* (Boston: Beacon Press, 1976), 3–26.

4. Sallie McFague, *Metaphorical Theology* (Philadelphia: Westminster Press, 1974), 145–92.

5. See Psalm 68:5, Psalm 89:26, Isaiah 9:6, Isaiah 63:16, and Jeremiah 3:19. Note that use of this name for the Divine was very rare in Hebrew scripture.

6. Sylvia Brinton Perera, *Descent to the Goddess: A Way of Initiation for Women* (Toronto: Inner City Books, 1981), 7–8.

7. Perera, *Descent to the Goddess,* 9.

8. Perera, *Descent to the Goddess,* 12.

9. Perera, *Descent to the Goddess,* 12.

10. Marian Woodman, *Addiction to Perfection: The Still Unravished Bride* (Toronto: Inner City Books, 1983), 55–57; *The Pregnant Virgin: a Process of Psychological Transformation* (Toronto: Inner City Books, 1985), 24–25, 37–40, 46–48.

11. From the title of a book by Christin Lore Weber, *Woman-Christ: A New Vision of Feminist Spirituality* (San Francisco: Harper & Row, 1987).

12. See Merlin Stone, *When God Was a Woman* (New York: Harcourt Brace Jovanovich, 1976) among others, for an understanding of the serpent in ancient Goddess religion and the Hebrew scriptural use of this symbol in its apologetic to bring people to adhere to the Hebrew religion.

13. See Rafael Patai, *The Hebrew Goddess,* 3d ed. (Detroit: Wayne State University, 1978), 96–111.

14. Interestingly, the image of the Holy Spirit in the story of Jesus' baptism (John 1:32) is that of the dove, an ancient Goddess symbol.

15. See Matthew 15:21–28 and Mark 7:24–30.

16. We see the feminine Divine in all persons who seek justice. This reference is to the grandmothers in Argentina who organized to search for children who had disappeared.

17. "He understood the Biblical number forty — the days of the flood, the years in the wilderness, Jesus' days of desert fasting. Each was an experience of creation out of chaos. And forty was chosen because that was the number of weeks in the womb. Meaning out of chaos" (From *Holy Week,* a novel by Paul Scott Wilson [Winfield, B.C.: WoodLake Books, 1984], 108).

18. The title "Jesus our Mother" is drawn from, among others, Julian of Norwich. See Brendan Doyle, *Meditations with Julian of Norwich* (Santa Fe, N.M.: Bear & Co., 1983), 99: "...Jesus is our true Mother in whom we are endlessly carried and out of whom we will never come."

19. For a perspective on the transition of ancient Goddess societies to patriarchy, see Merlin Stone, *When God Was a Woman* (San Diego: Harcourt Brace Jovanovich, 1976).

20. For detailed description of the Gospel portrayals of Jesus in relationship with women, see Leonard Swidler, *Biblical Affirmations of Woman* (Philadelphia: Westminster Press, 1979), 161–290.

21. Gabriele Uhlein, *Meditations with Hildegard of Bingen* (Santa Fe, N.M.: Bear & Co., 1982), 100.

22. See Patai, *The Hebrew Goddess,* for information about the Shekinah who was known as a Cloud, was said to speak like the sound of a bell, and who was believed to have accompanied the people of Israel in their exile (96–111).

23. See Patai, *The Hebrew Goddess,* for his discussion of the two figures of the Cherubim suggesting that in the secret mythology of the Israelite religion Yahweh was understood to have a spouse, who may at one time have been understood to be Asherah (67–95).

24. Barbara G. Walker, *The Crone: Woman of Age, Wisdom, and Power* (San Francisco: Harper and Row, 1985), 91–92.

25. Title of a book by Henri J. M. Nouwen, *The Wounded Healer* (New York: Doubleday, 1979).

26. "Our Passion for Justice" is the title of a book by Carter Heyward (New York: Pilgrim Press, 1984).

27. Patai, *The Hebrew Goddess,* cites the Talmud as saying that at the time of Moses' death the Shekinah carried him four miles to his secret place of burial (109).

28. See Elisabeth Moltmann-Wendell, *The Women around Jesus* (London: SCM Press, 1982), 15–60, for insights into the story of Martha and Mary.

29. For descriptions of women's ministry in the early Church, see Swidler, *Biblical Affirmations of Woman,* 290–356, and Elisabeth Schüssler Fiorenza, *In Memory of Her: A Feminist Theological Reconstruction of Christian Origins* (New York: Crossroad, 1984), 160–334.

30. Patai, *The Hebrew Goddess,* 103.

31. For a delineation of the feminine Divine as Shaddai, see Virginia Mollenkott, *The Divine Feminine* (New York: Crossroad, 1984), 54–59.

32. Patai, *The Hebrew Goddess,* 97–99.

33. See Rosemary Rader, *Breaking Boundaries: Male/Female Friendship in Early Christian Communities* (New York/Toronto: Paulist Press, 1983) for a description of women's role in the early monastic movement; and Rosemary Ruether, "Mothers of the Church: Ascetic Women in the Late Patristic Age" in Rosemary Ruether and Eleanor McLaughlin, eds., *Women of Spirit: Female Leadership in the Jewish and Christian Traditions* (New York: Simon and Schuster, 1979), 71–98.

34. See Eleanor McLaughlin, "Women, Power and the Pursuit of Holiness in Medieval Christianity" in Ruether and McLaughlin, eds., *Women of Spirit,* 99–130.

35. See Elaine C. Huber, " 'A Woman Must Not Speak,' " in Ruether and McLaughlin, eds., *Women of Spirit,* 153–79.

36. See Barbara Brown Zikmund, "The Feminist Thrust of Sectarian Christianity," in Ruether and McLaughlin, eds., *Women of Spirit,* 206–24.

37. From book title, Miriam Therese Winter, *WomanWord: A Feminist Lectionary and Psalter* (New York: Crossroad, 1991).

38. The expression "Cosmic homemaker" is used by Virginia Mollenkott in *The Feminine Divine,* 67.

39. *Webster's New World Thesaurus,* 388, 341, defines the title "Mistress" as a "woman in authority" or a "lady" in the sense of one who is the mistress of the estate.

40. See Swidler, *Biblical Affirmations of Woman,* for deutero-

Pauline ambivalence about the role of women regarding this passage
(337–38).

41. Walker, *The Crone*, 48–49. In ancient Goddess religion "blood
was the real essence of life and creation.... The Goddess not only
created the world out of her interior ocean of blood; she kept the very
gods alive with periodic infusions of this magic elixir, which Greeks
described as Mother Hera's supernatural red wine." The male sacrifice
with its shedding of blood was an attempt to participate in the power
of the Mother Goddess. See Robert Graves, *The White Goddess* (New
York: Vintage Books, 1958).

42. Walker, *The Crone*, 61–62. Shekinahs, originally tribal ances-
tresses, emanated the primordial Great Wisdom. See Jonas Hans, *The
Gnostic Religion* (Boston: Beacon Press, 1963).

43. Walker, *The Crone*, 57–58. The Crone's mythic ability to "kill
with a straight look" derived from the belief that she revealed the
mystery of herself only to the dying.

44. Walker, *The Crone*, 60.

45. Walker, *The Crone*, 45.

46. Phrase "original blessing" from Matthew Fox, from the book
with this title (Santa Fe, N.M.: Bear & Co., 1983).

47. Judith E. Sanderson, *The Women's Bible Commentary*, in Carole A. Newsom and Sharon H. Ringe, eds. (London: SPCK and
Louisville, Ky.: Westminster/John Knox Press, 1992), 226–27.

48. Patai, *The Hebrew Goddess*, 146.

49. Image expressed in song by Gordon Light, "She Flies On" in
Songs for a Gospel People (Winfield, B.C.: WoodLake Books, 1987),
126.

50. See Swidler, *Biblical Affirmations of Woman*, regarding the ne-
cessity for women to sacrifice their self-interest and their female blood
relationships in the interest of securing a male heir (118). See also
Rader, *Breaking Boundaries*, regarding the movement of women's
and men's monastic orders as liberation from the one option of
dependence upon the patriarchy for survival.

51. "World full of wonder," Eucharistic Prayer 5, Anglican Church
of Canada, *Book of Alternative Services* (Toronto: Anglican Book
Centre, 1985), 204.

Bibliography

Doyle, Brendan. *Meditations with Julian of Norwich*. Santa Fe, N.M.: Bear & Co., 1983.

Fox, Matthew. *Original Blessing*. Santa Fe, N.M.: Bear & Co., 1983.

General Synod of the Anglican Church of Canada. *The Book of Alternative Services*. Toronto: Anglican Book Centre, 1985.

Heyward, Carter. *Our Passion for Justice: Images of Power, Sexuality, and Liberation*. New York: Pilgrim Press, 1984.

Huber, Elaine C. "A Woman Must Not Speak." In Rosemary Ruether and Eleanor McLaughlin, eds. *Women of Spirit: Female Leadership in the Jewish and Christian Traditions* (New York: Simon and Schuster, 1979).

Laird, Charlton. *Webster's New World Thesaurus*. New York: New American Library, 1971.

Light, Gordon. "She Flies On." In *Songs for a Gospel People*. Winfield, B.C.: WoodLake Books, 1987.

McFague, Sallie. *Metaphorical Theology*. Philadelphia: Westminster Press, 1974.

McLaughlin, Eleanor. "Women, Power and the Pursuit of Holiness in Medieval Christianity." In Rosemary Ruether and Eleanor McLaughlin, eds. *Women of Spirit: Female Leadership in the Jewish and Christian Traditions*. New York: Simon and Schuster, 1979.

Miller, Jean Baker. *Toward a New Psychology of Women*. Boston: Beacon Press, 1976.

Mollenkott, Virginia Ramey. *The Divine Feminine: The Biblical Imagery of God as Female*. New York: Crossroad, 1984.

Moltmann-Wendell, Elisabeth. *The Women around Jesus*. London: SCM Press, 1982.

Nouwen, Henri J. M. *The Wounded Healer.* New York: Doubleday, 1979.

Patai, Rafael. *The Hebrew Goddess,* 3rd enlarged ed. Detroit: Wayne State University, 1990.

Perera, Sylvia Brinton. *Descent to the Goddess: A Way of Initiation for Women.* Toronto: Inner City Books, 1981.

Rader, Rosemary. *Breaking Boundaries: Male/Female Friendship in Early Christian Communities.* New York: Paulist, 1983.

Ruether, Rosemary. "Mothers of the Church: Ascetic Women in the Late Patristic Age." In Rosemary Ruether and Eleanor McLaughlin, eds. *Women of Spirit: Female Leadership in the Jewish and Christian Traditions.* New York: Simon and Schuster, 1979.

Sanderson, Judith E. "Zephaniah." In Carole A. Newsom and Sharon H. Ringe, eds. *The Women's Bible Commentary.* London: SPCK and Louisville, Ky.: Westminster/John Knox Press, 1992.

Schüssler Fiorenza, Elisabeth. *In Memory of Her: A Feminist Theological Reconstruction of Christian Origins.* New York: Crossroad, 1984.

Swidler, Leonard. *Biblical Affirmations of Woman.* Philadelphia: Westminster Press, 1979.

Uhlein, Gabriele. *Meditations with Hildegard of Bingen.* Santa Fe, N.M.: Bear & Co., 1982.

Walker, Barbara G. *The Crone: Woman of Age, Wisdom, and Power.* San Francisco: Harper & Row, 1985.

Weber, Christin Lore. *WomanChrist: A New Vision of Feminist Spirituality.* San Francisco: Harper & Row, 1987.

Winter, Miriam Therese. *WomanWisdom: A Feminist Lectionary and Psalter.* New York: Crossroad, 1991.

———. *WomanWord: A Feminist Lectionary and Psalter.* New York: Crossroad, 1991.

Woodman, Marian. *Addiction to Perfection: The Still Unravished Bride.* Toronto: Inner City Books, 1983.

———. *The Pregnant Virgin: A Process of Psychological Transformation.* Toronto: Inner City Books, 1985.

Zikmund, Barbara Brown. "The Feminist Thrust of Sectarian Christianity." In Rosemary Ruether and Eleanor McLaughlin, eds. *Women of Spirit: Female Leadership in the Jewish and Christian Traditions* (New York: Simon and Schuster, 1979).

Index of Biblical References

— ℘ —

142